Children of the Wild. With Illustrations by Paul Bransom

CHILDREN OF THE WILD

THE MACMILLAN COMPANY
NEW YORK · BOSTON · CHICAGO
DALLAS · ATLANTA · SAN FRANCISCO

MACMILLAN & CO., LIMITED
LONDON · BOMBAY · CALCUTTA
MELBOURNE

THE MACMILLAN CO. OF CANADA, LTD.
TORONTO

"He reached around....and pulled with all his might."

CHILDREN OF THE WILD

BY

CHARLES G. D. ROBERTS

AUTHOR OF "KINGS IN EXILE," "THE FEET OF THE FURTIVE," ETC.

WITH ILLUSTRATIONS
BY PAUL BRANSOM

New York
THE MACMILLAN COMPANY
1921

Set up and electrotyped. Published September, 1913

CONTENTS

LIST OF ILLUSTRATIONS

FACING PAGE

CHILDREN OF THE WILD

Children of the Wild

I

THE LITTLE FURRY ONES THAT SLIDE DOWN HILL

In the brown, balsam-smelling log cabin on the shores of Silverwater, loveliest and loneliest of wilderness lakes, the Babe's great thirst for information seemed in a fair way to be satisfied. Young as he was, and city-born, the lure of the wild had nevertheless already caught him, and the information that he thirsted for so insatiably was all about the furred or finned or feathered kindreds of the wild. And here by Silverwater, alone with his Uncle Andy and big Bill Pringle, the guide, his natural talent for asking questions was not so firmly discouraged as it was at home.

But even thus early in this adventurous career, this fascinating and never-ending quest of knowledge, the Babe found himself confronted by a most difficult problem. He had to choose between authorities. He had to select between information and information. He had to differentiate for himself between what Bill told him and what his Uncle Andy told him. He was a serious-minded child, who had already passed through that most painful period of doubt as to Santa Claus and the Fairies, and had not yet reached the period of certainty about everything. He was capable of both belief and doubt. So, naturally, he had his difficulties.

Bill certainly knew an astonishing lot about the creatures of the wild. But also, like all guides who are worth their salt, he knew an astonishing lot of things that weren't so. He had imagination, or he would never have done for a guide. When he knew—which was not often—that he did *not* know a thing, he could put two and two together and make it yield the most extraordinary results. He felt it one of his first duties to be interesting. And above all, he felt it his duty to be infallible. No one could be expected to have implicit faith in a guide who was not infallible. He never acknowledged insufficient information about anything whatever that pertained to the woods and waters. Also he had a very poor opinion of what others might profess to know. He felt convinced that so long as he refrained from any *too* lively contributions to the science of animal life, no one would be able to discredit him. But he was conscientious in his deductions. He would never have permitted himself to say that blue herons wore gum boots in wading, just because he had happened to find an old gum boot among the reeds by the outlet of the lake, where the herons did most of their fishing. He remembered that that gum boot was one of a pair which had been thrown away by a former visitor to Silverwater.

Uncle Andy, on the other hand, knew that there was an astonishing lot *he didn't* know about animals, and he didn't hesitate to say so. He was a reformed sportsman, who, after spending a great part of his life in happily killing things all over the earth, had come to the quaint conclusion that most of them were more interesting alive than dead, especially to themselves. He found a kindred spirit in the

Babe, whose education, along the lines of maiming cats and sparrows with sling shot or air gun, had been absolutely neglected.

Uncle Andy was wont to say that there was only one man in all the world who knew *all* about *all* the animals—and that he was not Andrew Barton, Esq. At this, Bill would smile proudly. At first this modesty on Uncle Andy's part was a disappointment to the Babe. But it ended in giving him confidence in whatever Uncle Andy told him; especially after he came to realize that when Uncle Andy spoke of the only man in the world who knew *all* about animals, he *did* not mean Bill.

But though the whole field of animal lore was one of absorbing interest to the Babe, from the day when he was so fortunate as to witness a mother fish-hawk teaching her rather unwilling and unventuresome young ones to fly, it was his fellow babes of the wild that he was most anxious to hear about. In this department of woods lore, Bill was so deeply ignorant that, not caring to lean *too* heavily on his imagination, lest it should break and stick into him, he used to avoid it quite obstinately. He would say—"Them youngsters is all alike, anyhow, an' it ain't worth while to waste no time a-studyin' 'em!" So here Uncle Andy had the field all to himself. Whenever he undertook to enlighten the Babe on any such subject, Bill would go off somewhere and scornfully chop down trees.

* * * * * * *

Silverwater was fed by many brooks from the deep-wooded surrounding hills. Toward one of these, on a certain golden afternoon, Uncle Andy and the Babe were betaking themselves along the shadowy trail, where the green-brown moss was soft under foot and their careful steps made no noise. When they spoke it was in quiet undertones; for the spirit of the woods was on the Babe, and he knew that by keeping very quiet there was always the chance of surprising some fascinating mystery.

The two were going fishing—for Uncle Andy, with a finely human inconsistency, was an enthusiastic fisherman, and the stream toward which they were making their way was one of deep pools and cool "stillwaters" where the biggest fish were wont to lie during the hot weather. Uncle Andy had a prejudice against those good people who were always sternly consistent, and he was determined that he would never allow himself to become a crank; so he went on enthusiastically killing fish with the same zest that he had once brought to the hunting of beast and bird.

While they were yet several hundred yards from the stream, suddenly there came to their ears, unmistakable though muffled by the intervening trees, the sound of a brisk splash, as if something had fallen into the water. Uncle Andy stopped short in his tracks, motionless as a setter marking his bird. The Babe stopped likewise, faithfully imitating him. A couple of seconds later came another splash, as heavy as the first; and then, in quick succession, two lighter ones.

For a moment or two the Babe kept silence, though bursting with curiosity. Then he whispered tensely—"What's that?"

"Otter," replied Uncle Andy, in a murmur as soft as the wind in the sedge-tops.

"Why?" continued the Babe, meaning to say—"But what on earth are they doing?" and trusting that Uncle Andy would appreciate the self-restraint of the monosyllable.

"Sliding down hill," muttered Uncle Andy, without turning his head. Then, holding up his hand as a sign that there were to be no more questions asked, he crept forward noiselessly; and the Babe followed at his heels.

After two or three minutes the sounds were repeated in the same succession as before—first two heavy splashes, and then two lighter ones. Unable to ask questions, the Babe was obliged to think for himself.

He had only a vague idea what otters were like, but he knew a good deal about sliding down hill. He pictured to himself a high, rough bank leading down to the water; but as not even Bill's daring imagination would have represented the gamesome beasts as employing toboggans or hand-sleds, he thought it must be rather bumpy and uncomfortable work coasting over the roots and rocks on one's own unprotected anatomy.

The sounds continued, growing louder and louder, till the two adventurers must have been within thirty or forty feet of the stream; and they were creeping as noiselessly as a shadow slips over the grass, in the hope of catching the merrymakers at their game. But suddenly there came one great splash, heavy and prolonged, as if all the sliders had come down close together. And then silence. Uncle Andy crouched motionless for several minutes, as if he had been turned into a stump. Then he straightened himself up with a disappointed air.

"Gone!" he muttered. "Cleared out! They've heard us or smelt us!"

"Oh!" exclaimed the Babe in a voice of deep concern; though, as a matter of fact, he was immensely relieved, the strain of the prolonged tension and preternatural stillness having begun to make him feel that he must make a noise or burst.

Two minutes later they came out on the banks of the stream.

The stream at this point was perhaps twenty-five feet in width, deep, dark, and almost without current. Only by noting the bend of the long watergrasses could one tell which way it ran. The hither bank was low and grassy, with a fallen trunk slanting out into the water. But the shore opposite was some twelve or fifteen feet high, very steep, and quite naked, having been cut by the floods from a ridge of clay. Down the middle of this incline a narrow track had been worn so smooth that it gleamed in the sun almost like ice.

As he stared across the water a dozen questions crowded to the Babe's lips. But he realized in time that the answers to them were fairly obvious to himself, and he heroically choked them back. Had he not that very morning been rebuked by his uncle for asking too many of what he called "footy" questions? But one burst forth now, in spite of himself.

"What do they do it for?" he demanded—having perhaps a vague idea that all the motives of the wild creatures were, or ought to be, purely utilitarian.

Uncle Andy turned upon him a withering look; and he shifted his feet uneasily, convicted of another "footy" question.

"What do you slide down hill for?" inquired Uncle Andy sarcastically.

"Oh!" said the Babe hastily. "I see. And now are we going to catch some fish?"

But Uncle Andy had stood his rod in a bush and sat down on the fallen tree; and now he was getting out his old black pipe.

"Well now," he answered presently, "I don't

think it would be much use trying. What do *you* think?"

"Of course not," answered the Babe. "Otter have scared 'em all away."

"You really are doing very well," said Uncle Andy, "if you *did* ask that one fool question. When we were creeping up on the otter, to try and get a look at them while they were playing, you did very well indeed. You stepped as light as a cat, and that's not easy mind, I tell you, when one's not trained to it. You didn't even breathe too hard—and I know you must have been just bursting with excitement. You've got the makings of a first-rate woodsman in you, if you take pains."

The Babe's small chest swelled with pride; for commendation from Uncle Andy was a scarce article. He too sat down on the fallen trunk and began digging at the bark with his knife to hide his exultation.

"I suppose now," went on Uncle Andy presently, when his pipe was drawing well, "you know quite a lot about otter."

"Nothing at all but what Bill's told me," answered the Babe with fine diplomacy.

"Forget it!" said Uncle Andy; and went on

smoking in thoughtful silence. Presently he remarked—"This otter family appears to have been having a pretty good time!"

"Great!" said the Babe laconically.

"Well," continued Uncle Andy, regarding him with approval, "there was once another otter family, away up on the Little North Fork of the Ottanoonsis, that used to have such good times till at last they struck a streak of bad luck."

"Did you know them?" asked the Babe.

"Well, not as you might say intimately," answered Uncle Andy, with a far-away look in his grey eyes. "You see, they had no way of knowing how nice I was, so they never admitted me into their family circle. But I knew a lot more about them than they ever guessed, I can tell you. When the flies weren't too bad I used to lie by the hour behind a thick bush, never stirring a finger, and watch them."

"My, but how tired you must have got!" interrupted the Babe feelingly.

"I don't *have* to twiddle my fingers, and scratch my head, and jump up and down every two minutes and a half," said Uncle Andy rather severely. "But, as I was going to say, they also got used to seeing me sitting on the bank, quiet and harmless, till they no longer felt so shy of me as they did of Jim Cringle, my guide. They knew Jim was an enemy, and they gave him a wide berth always. But they seemed to think I wasn't of much account."

"Oh!" protested the Babe politely. It did not seem to him quite right that Uncle Andy should be regarded lightly, even by an otter.

"Well, you know, I *wasn't* of much account. I was neither dangerous, like Jim Cringle, nor good to eat, like a muskrat or a pickerel. So I don't appear any more in this yarn. If you find yourself wondering how I came to know about some of the things I'm going to tell you, just make believe I got it from the chickadee, who is the most confidential little chap in the world, or from the whisky-Jack, who makes a point, as you may have observed, of knowing everybody else's business."

"Or from Jim Cringle?" inquired the Babe demurely.

But Uncle Andy only frowned. He always discouraged the Babe's attempts at raillery.

"The two Little Furry Ones," he continued,

after pressing down the tobacco in his pipe, "were born in a dry, warm, roomy den in the bank, under the roots of an old birch that slanted out over the water. The front door was deep under water. But as the old otters had few enemies to dread, being both brave and powerful, they had also a back entrance on dry land, hidden by a thicket of fir bushes. The two furry 'pups' were at first as sprawling and helpless as newborn kittens, though of course a good deal bigger than any kittens *you* have ever seen. And being so helpless, their father and mother never left them alone. One always stayed with them while the other went away to hunt trout or muskrat."

"Why, what *could* get at them in there?" interrupted the Babe.

"You see," explained Uncle Andy graciously, "either a fox or a weasel *might* come in by the back door—if they were hungry enough to take the risk. Or what was much more likely, that slim, black, murderous robber, the mink, might come swimming in by the front entrance, pop his narrow, cruel head above the water, see the youngsters alone, and be at their throats in a twinkling. The old otters, who were very devoted parents, were not running any risks like that, I can tell you."

"I guess not!" agreed the Babe, wagging his head wisely.

"Well," went on Uncle Andy, "just *because* those level-headed old otters were always ready for it, nothing happened. You'd better make a note of that. If you are always ready for trouble when the other fellow makes it, he will be pretty shy about beginning. That's why the foxes and the weasels and the minks never came around.

"When the Little Furry Ones were about the size of five months' kittens they were as handsome a pair of youngsters as you are ever likely to set eyes upon. Their fur, rich and soft and dark, was the finest ever seen. Like their parents, they had bodies shaped for going through the water at a tremendous speed —built like a bulldog's for strength, and like an eel's for suppleness."

"Not *slimy!*" protested the Babe, who had hated eels whole-heartedly ever since the day when he had tried to take one off the hook.

"Of course not!" answered Uncle Andy impatiently. "As I was going to say, they were shaped a good deal like those seals you've seen in the Zoo, only that instead of flippers they had regulation legs and feet, and also a tail. It was a tail worth having, too, and not merely intended for ornament. It was very thick at the base and tapering, something like a lizard's, and so powerful that one twist of it could drive its owner through the water like a screw."

"Wish I could swim that way!" murmured the Babe, trying to do the movement, as he imagined it, with his legs.

"But though the Little Furry Ones were just built for swimming," continued Uncle Andy, graciously overlooking the interruption, "they were actually afraid of it. They liked to see their father or their mother dive smoothly down into the clear, goldy-brown water of their front door, and out into that patch of yellow sunlight shimmering on the weedy bottom. But when invited to follow, they drew back into the corner and pretended to be terribly busy.

"One fine morning, however, to their great delight they were led out by the back door, under the bush, and introduced to the outside world. How huge and strange it looked to them! For a few minutes they stole about on their absurdly short, sturdy legs, poking their noses into everything, and jumping back startled at the strange smells they encountered; while their parents, lying down nearby, watched them lazily. At last, beginning to feel more at home in this big, airy world, they fell to romping with each other on the sunny bank, close beside the water. Presently their parents got up and came over beside them. The father slipped gracefully in, and began diving, darting this way and that, and throwing himself half-way out of the water. It was most interesting, I can tell you, and the two little Furry Ones stopped their play, at the very edge of the bank, to watch him. But when he called to them coaxingly to come in with him and try it, they turned away their heads and pretended to think it wasn't worth looking at after all. They would rather look at the trees and the sky, and kept staring up at them as if perfectly fascinated. And *while* they were staring upwards in this superior way, they got a great surprise. Their mother slily slipped her nose under them and threw them, one after the other, far out into the water."

"Ow!" exclaimed the Babe with a little gasp of sympathy. He himself felt the shock of that sudden, chill plunge.

Uncle Andy chuckled.

"That's just the way they felt," said he. "When they came to the top again they found, to their surprise, that they could swim; and feeling most indignant and injured they struck out straight for shore. But there, between them and the good dry ground, swam their mother, and would not let them land. They did not see how mothers could be so heartless. But there was no help for it; so they swam out again very haughtily and joined their father in mid-stream. And before they knew it they were enjoying themselves immensely.

"And now life became much more interesting to them. For a bit it was harder to keep them out of the water than it had been to get them into it. They had their first lessons in fishing. And though they were too clumsy at first to catch even a slow, mud-grubbing sucker, they found the attempt most interesting. The stream just opposite their home was deep and quiet, but a little way below, the current ran strong; and once, having ridden down it gaily for a couple of hundred yards, they found themselves unable to swim back against it. At first they battled bravely and were most surprised to find themselves making so little progress. Then they grew tired; and then frightened, and they were just being carried off down stream by this strange, soft, irresistible force when their mother arrived. The current was nothing to her. She took them on her back, and shot off up stream again with them. After that they would ride on her back, or on their father's whenever they got tired. And their parents began to take them on long trips up and down stream. You see, their housekeeping being so simple, they didn't mind going away even for a couple of days at a time, and leaving the house to look after itself."

"I don't think I'd like to be wet like that *all* the time, even in summer," remarked the Babe, shaking his head thoughtfully.

"Oh, they weren't that. They used to go ashore and, in spite of their ridiculously short legs, make most respectably long journeys through the woods to some other stream, pretending, I suppose, that the fish over there had a different flavor. Sometimes, too, when they came upon a patch of smooth, mossy ground, they would have a wild romp, as if they had just been let out of school—a sort of game of tag, in which the father and mother played just as hard as the youngsters. Or they would have a regular tug of war, pulling on opposite ends of a stick, till the moss was all torn up as if a little cyclone had loafed along that way. Then one day they came to a clay bank, something like that one across yonder. The old ones had been there before, but not for some time, and the clay had got all dry and hard. But the father and mother knew very well how to fix that. When they had slid down a couple of times with their fur all dripping the track was smooth as oil. As for the youngsters, you may depend upon it they did not need any coaxing or persuasion to make them believe *that* was a good game."

"I should think not!" murmured the Babe, looking longingly over the stream to where the wet slide glistened in the sun, and wishing that he might try it without any regard whatever to the seat of his little trousers.

"Taking it all together it was a pretty jolly life, I can tell you, there in the sweet-smelling, shadowy woods and sunny waters. Then one day all at once, as quick as falling off a log, everything was changed."

Uncle Andy paused to relight his pipe. After a few seconds the Babe's impatience got the better of him; and before he could stop himself he blurted out "Why?" The moment he had spoken he knew it was a fool question to ask, and he flushed. But to his grateful relief Uncle did not seem to hear.

"A hunter from the city came that way. He had a good eye, a repeating rifle, and no imagination whatever. With the luck that sometimes comes to those fellows, he was sitting under a tree near the bank, staring across at the otter-slide (which did not mean anything whatever or suggest anything to him, but was merely a strip of bare clay), when the otter family came to slide. The father started down. It was most interesting—so the stranger under the tree, who was as spry as a sparrowhawk, shot instantly; and the otter came

"He saw that the otter children had grown too big for him."

down in a crumpled heap. The mother might have escaped; but for just one second she hesitated, glancing round to see if her little ones were out of danger. That second was enough for the smart shot across the water. She dropped. It was good shooting, of course. The two little ones, horrified by the spiteful noise, and quite unable to understand what had happened, shrank away into some thick bushes and lay very still, waiting for their mother to come and tell them the danger was past."

"And she could never come!" murmured the Babe thoughtfully.

"Well, she didn't," snorted Uncle Andy, the discourager of sentiment. Fairly reeking with sentiment himself, at heart, he disliked all manifestation of it in himself or others. He liked it left to the imagination. "They never stirred for an hour or more," he went on. "Then at last they stole out and began looking everywhere for those lost parents. All about the slide they hunted—among the bushes at the top, in the water and the rushes at the bottom—but they found nothing. For the man had come in his canoe and carried off his victims.

"All day long the two Little Furry Ones continued their search. But you would not have known them for the same creatures as those which had started out that morning. Then they had played carelessly and gone boldly, thinking not of enemies and fearing none. Now they crept noiselessly, sniffing this way and that, and never showing their noses outside a thicket without first taking observations. For life was now a very different matter with them. Never in all their lives before had they come across so many hostile and threatening smells as they encountered this one afternoon. But then, to be sure, they had never looked for them before. They were all the time running into trails of mink, or weasel, or wildcat; and it seemed to them as if the world had suddenly become quite full of foxes. They were painfully surprised, for they had never thought there were so many disagreeable creatures in the world. You see, being so young and inexperienced, it never occurred to them that one fox or one weasel could make quite a lot of trails. So they kept having palpitations every other minute.

"It was just as well, however, that they got

such an exaggerated idea of the numbers of their enemies. For it was astonishing how quickly the news got around that the old otters were dead. Toward sunset that evening, when the two lonely youngsters, puzzled and miserable, stole back to their old den under the bank, they found that a mink had dared to kill a big trout in their own pool. There were the remains, and the presumptuous intruder's tracks, almost at their very door. They were indignant, and the thick hair bristled on their necks. But, realizing suddenly how hungry they were, they did not scorn to eat the stranger's leavings. Then they dived into their den; and after sniffing about and whimpering lonesomely for a while, they curled themselves up close together and went to sleep. It had been a strange and dreadful day.

"As you may imagine, these two youngsters had never yet been trained to the useful habit of sleeping with one ear open. They had left that to their parents. But to-night, even while they slept most soundly, something within them seemed to keep watch. Whatever it was, suddenly it woke them. And instantly they were tremendously wide awake. Before they knew why they did it, they were uncurled from the ball in which they slept and, crouching side by side, glaring savagely up the narrow passage that led to their back door.

"There they saw a pair of cruel eyes, small and flaming, and set very close together, which seemed to float slowly down towards them."

Here Uncle Andy was so inconsiderate as to pause, as if he wanted to think. The Babe could not hold himself in.

"Was it a snake?" he demanded breathlessly.

"There you go again, interrupting," growled Uncle Andy, most unfairly. "And who ever heard of a snake's eyes flaming? But the Little Furry Ones knew what it was at once; and the hair stood straight up on their necks. Of course they were frightened a little. But most of all were they in a rage at such an impudent intrusion. There was no sign of fear, I can tell you, in the low growl which came from between their long, white, snarling teeth. And those stealthy eyes halted. For half a minute, motionless, they studied the crouching and defiant youngsters, evidently surprised to see how big and strong they had grown. Then, very slowly and with dignity, they withdrew and presently disappeared. For the weasel, though perhaps the most fearless assassin that prowls the woods, is no fool. And he saw that the otter children had grown too big for him to handle.

"The youngsters were a good deal set up, of course, by this unexpectedly easy rebuff of so venomous an enemy; but there was no more thought of sleep for them. It made them terribly anxious, the idea of anything stealing in on them that way, by the back door. For a long time they lay there motionless, their wide eyes staring into the dark, their ears straining to every faint, mysterious sound, their sensitive noses questioning every scent that came breathing in to them from the still night forest. At last they heard a stealthy footfall outside the back door. It was as light—oh, lighter than a falling leaf. But *they* heard it. If you and I had such ears as that, maybe we could hear the grasses growing."

"*That* would be fun," muttered the Babe.

"And then," continued Uncle Andy, "they smelt a faint, musky scent. I *don't* think it would be fun if we had such noses as that. We'd smell so many smells we did not want to.

Eh? And I tell you, the youngsters did not want to smell *that* smell. It was a fox. They couldn't fight a fox. Not yet. With their hearts in their throats they backed softly down to the front door, and waited, ready to slip into the water.

"But fortunately the fox was cunning, and proud of it. He had heard a rumor that the old otters were dead. But he was much too cunning to believe all he heard. It would be just like them, he thought, to pretend they were dead, so that he might come in and get caught. Assuredly there was a good, strong, live otter smell coming up out of that hole. He poked his nose down and gave a very loud sniff, then cocked his ear sharply and listened. Nothing stirred. Had it been only the little ones, down there all by themselves, he thought, they would have been frightened enough to jump. So, it was plainly a trap. Waving his great bushy tail complaisantly, he tiptoed off to hunt rabbits, pleased with the notion that somebody else was going to get taken in.

"The youngsters stayed where they were, close beside the water. The first glimmer of dawn, striking on the misty surface of the pool outside, struggled up into the den. The youngsters turned to greet it, with the thought, perhaps, that it was time to go fishing. Just at this moment the mink, who had been looking for the remnants of his trout where he had left them on the bank (he was a fool, of course, ever to have left them there), came diving into the deep front door of the den to avenge himself on the unprotected little ones. His slim black form was visible as it rose through the greying water. As the pointed head popped above the surface, it was confronted by two grinning heads which snarled savagely in its face and snapped at it in fearless defiance. The mink was surprised and pained. He had expected to find those two youngsters huddled together and already half frightened to death just at being alone. He had *not* expected to find them half so big. In fact, there at home, and guarding their own domain, they looked to him much bigger than they really were. A very small man, you know, may look about seven feet high when he stands in his own door and tells you to keep out. Eh, what? Well, the mink suddenly felt sort of bashful about intruding. He discreetly withdrew, without thinking to make inquiry about the fish. And his sudden diffidence was very fortunate for the two Little Furry Ones. For the mink, let me tell you, would have been a tough proposition for them to tackle.

"This sudden departure of the terrible mink made the two youngsters feel almost bigger than was good for them. But the otter, fortunately, is born cautious, no matter how courageous he may be. So the youngsters were not spoiled by their good luck. They waited a few minutes, to give the mink a chance to get good and far away. Then they dived forth into the misty pool. Never before had they seen one quarter so many fish in it. They breakfasted very well on a couple of plump, silvery chub—though they would have preferred trout, of course—and then, just for sport, began killing as many as they could, only swallowing a bite out of each, from the thick, flaky meat behind the head. They were young, you see—though not more foolish than lots of sportsmen we hear about. In a very few minutes, of course, every fish that could get away had got away as far as possible from that deadly pool. And then the two reckless fishermen crawled ashore and began a tug of war with a stick. They could just not help playing, you see, any more than kittens or puppies could; though they were still lonely and anxious. And in their play they kept very close to the water's edge, in case the fox should happen along to inquire after their parents.

"The fox did not turn up. But after some time they caught sight of a great, dark bird winnowing his way slowly above the tree tops. Just to be on the safe side, they got into the water so quickly that one of them, to save time, threw himself in backwards. They did not know that it was only a fishhawk, an amiable soul, quite indifferent to such delicacies as young otters. Another thing they did not know was that if the fishhawk *had* wanted them, he could have caught them more comfortably in the water than on shore.

"When the great bird was well out of sight they started off down stream, partly to have another look for their lost parents, partly because they had nothing better to do. But they did not go very far that day, or have any more very exciting adventures. They spent most of their time in the water, where they had no foe to watch out for except the mink. And, as the fish had now learned to beware of them, they had enough to do in satisfying their lively appetites. That night they slept in the den, lying close to the water's edge, lest the fox should come. And they had no visitors.

"The next day they were feeling more confident, more sure of themselves. So they set out on a longer expedition. In the course of the morning they killed a big muskrat, after a sharp fight, and felt terribly proud of themselves. They got bitten, of course, and had their fur all mussed up, so it meant a long, elaborate toilet in the warm grass by the water's edge. And it was not till early in the afternoon that they came once more to the fateful slide where their parents had so mysteriously vanished.

"At the sight of it, as they came upon it suddenly around a bend of the stream, their fur bristled and they crouched flat, glancing angrily this way and that. Then they stole forward, and once more explored the whole place minutely. At last, finding nothing to alarm them, in an absent-minded way one of the two went down the slide, splash into the cool brown water. The other followed at once. The temptation was simply not to be resisted, you know. And in a minute more they were both hard at it, having the time of their lives—hawks, foxes, minks, and vanished parents alike forgotten."

"Oh!" protested the Babe in a shocked voice.

"You may say 'Oh!'" retorted Uncle Andy, "but let me tell you, if the wild creatures hadn't pretty short memories, they would have a very unhappy time.

"Well, they had been enjoying themselves and forgetting their troubles for some little time, when, just as it came down the slide, one of them was grabbed and pulled under. The mink had arrived and decided to settle accounts with the youngsters. He had probably been thinking it over, and come to the conclusion that they were getting too bumptious. Darting up through the water, he had snapped savagely at the careless player's throat.

"But the latter—it was the female, and spry, I can tell you—had felt that darting terror even before she had time to see it, and twisted aside like an eel. So instead of catching her by the throat, as he had so amiably intended, the mink only got her leg, up close by the shoulder. It was a deep and merciless grip; but instead of squealing—which she could not have done anyhow, being already under water—the Little Furry One just sank her sharp white teeth into the back of her enemy's neck, and held on for dear life. It was *exactly* the right thing to do, though she did not know it. For she had got her grip so high up on the mink's neck that he could not twist his head around far enough to catch her by the throat. Deep down at the bottom of the pool the two rolled over and over each other; and the mink was most annoyed to find how strong the youngster was, and how set in her ways. Moreover, he had been under water longer than she had, and was beginning to feel he'd like a breath of fresh air. He gave a kick with his powerful hind legs, and, as the Little Furry One had no objection, up they came.

"Now, the other youngster had not been able, just at first, to make out what was happening. He thought his sister had gone down to the bottom for fun. But when he saw her coming up, locked in that deadly struggle with their old enemy, his heart swelled with fury.

When the struggling pair reached the surface, lashing and splashing—"

He sprang clear out into the deep water when the struggling pair reached the surface, lashing and splashing, and the mink had only bare time to snatch a single breath of air before he found another adversary on his back, and was borne down inexorably to the bottom.

"Just about this time a perfectly new idea flashed across the mink's mind, and it startled him. For the first time in his life he thought that perhaps he was a fool. Young otters seemed to be so much older than he had imagined them, so much more unreasonable and bad-tempered, and to have so many teeth. It was a question, he decided—while he was being mauled around among the water weeds—that would bear some thinking over. He wanted to think about it right away. There was no time like the present for digesting these new ideas. Seeing a big root sticking out of the bank, close to the bottom, with a tremendous effort he clawed himself under it and scraped off his antagonists. Shooting out on the other side, he darted off like an eel through the water grass, and hurried away up stream to a certain hollow log he knew, where he might lick his bites and meditate undisturbed.

The two Little Furry Ones stared after him for a moment, then crawled out upon the bank and lay down in the sunny grass."

Uncle Andy got up with an air of decision. "Let's go catch some fish," he said. "They ought to be beginning to rise about now, over by Spring Brook."

"But what became of the two Little Furry Ones after that?" demanded the Babe, refusing to stir.

"Well, *now,*" protested Uncle Andy in an injured voice, "you *know* I ain't like Bill and some other folk. I don't know everything. But I've every reason to believe that, with any kind of otter luck, they lived to grow up and have families of their own—and taught every one of them, you may be sure, to slide down hill. As likely as not, that very slide over yonder belongs to one of their families. Now come along and don't ask any more questions."

CHAPTER II

THE BLACK IMPS OF PINE-TOP

"I THINK I'd *like* to be a bird," murmured the Babe, wistfully gazing up at the dark green, feathery top of the great pine, certain of whose branches were tossing and waving excitedly against the blue, although there was not a breath of wind to ruffle the expanse of Silverwater. "I *think* I'd like it—rather." He added the qualification as a prudent afterthought, lest Uncle Andy should think him foolish.

"In *summer!*" suggested Uncle Andy, following the Babe's eyes toward the agitated pine-top.

"Of *course* in summer!" corrected the Babe hastily. "It must be awful to be a bird in winter!" And he shuddered.

"You'd better not say 'of course' in that confident way," said Uncle Andy rather severely. "You know so many of the birds go away south in the winter; and they manage to have a pretty jolly time of it, I should think."

For a moment the Babe looked abashed. Then his face brightened.

"But then, it *is* summer, for *them*, isn't it?" said he sweetly.

Uncle Andy gave him a suspicious look, to see if he realized the success of his retort. "Had me there!" he thought to himself. But the Babe's face betrayed no sign of triumph, nothing but that eager appetite for information of which Uncle Andy so highly approved.

"So it depends on what kind of a bird, eh, what?" said he, deftly turning the point. Then he scratched a sputtering sulphur match on the long-suffering leg of his trousers.

"Yes," said the Babe, with more decision now. "I'd like to be a crow."

Uncle Andy smoked meditatively for several minutes before replying, till the Babe began to grow less confident as to the wisdom of his choice. But as he gazed up at those green pine-tops, so clear against the blue, all astir with black wings and gay, excited *ca*-ings, he took courage again. Certainly *those* crows, at least, were enjoying themselves immensely.

And he had always had a longing to be able to play in the tops of the trees.

"Well, said Uncle Andy at last, "perhaps you're not so *very* far off, this time. If I couldn't be an eagle, or a hawk, or a wild goose, or one of those big-horned owls that we hear every night, or a humming-bird, then I'd rather be a crow than most. A crow has got enemies, of course, but then he's got brains, so that he knows how to make a fool of most of his enemies. And he certainly does manage to get a lot of fun out of life, taking it all in all, except when the owl comes gliding around his roosting places in the black nights, or an extra bitter midwinter frost catches him after a rainy thaw."

He paused and drew hard on his pipe, with that far-away look in his eyes which the Babe had learned to regard as the forerunner to a story. There were some interesting questions to ask, of course; but though bursting with curiosity as to why anyone should find it better to be a wild goose, or even a humming-bird, than a crow, the Babe sternly repressed himself. He would ask those questions by and by, that he promised himself. But he had learned that to speak inopportunely was sometimes to make Uncle Andy change his mind and shut up like an oyster. He was determined that he would not open his mouth till the story should be well under way, till his uncle should be himself too much interested to be willing to stop. And then, to his horror, just as he was recording this sagacious resolution in his mind, he heard himself demanding:

"But *why* after a rainy thaw?"

It was out before he could choke it back. There was nothing for him to do but stick to it and gaze at his uncle with disarming innocence. Uncle Andy turned upon him a glance of slow contumely.

"If you were going to be caught out in a blizzard, would you rather be in dry clothes or in wet ones?" he inquired.

The Babe smiled apologetically and resumed his study of the agitated pine-tops, whence, from time to time, a crow, or two or three, would burst forth for a brief, whirling flight, as if to show how it was done. Then other flights were made, which seemed to the Babe extremely brief and hesitating, as if the flyers were nervous when they found themselves out clear of the branches and suspended on their own wings over the empty deeps of air. Presently there was a sudden tumultuous outburst of *ca*-ing, the branches shook, and a whole flock, perhaps two score or more, swarmed into the air. After a few moments of clamorous confusion they all flew off in the direction of the muddy flats at the lower end of the lake. The pine-tops subsided into stillness. But an occasional hoarse croak or muttered guttural showed that a few of their occupants had been left at home. The Babe wondered what it had all been about, but he succeeded in holding his tongue.

In a moment or two this heroic self-restraint had its reward.

"Trying to show some of the youngsters how to fly, and jeering at the timid ones and the stupid ones!" explained Uncle Andy.

"Oh!" said the Babe, with a long, appreciative inflection.

Uncle Andy paused, leaving an opening for more questions. But the Babe refused to be drawn, so presently, with a comprehending grin, he went on:

"It's rather a small affair for crows, you

know, this colony of theirs here on Silverwater. I suppose they've been crowded out from the places they really prefer, along the skirts of the settlements on the other side of the Ridge. They would rather live always somewhere near the farms and the cleared fields. Not that they have any special affection for man. Far from it. They dislike him, and distrust him, and seem to think him a good deal of a fool, too. His so-called 'scarecrows' are a great joke to them, and have been known at times to afford some fine materials for the lining of their nests. But they find him so useful in many really important ways that they establish their colonies in his neighborhood whenever they possibly can."

Here Uncle Andy made another long pause. He looked at the Babe suspiciously.

"Is anything the matter?" he demanded.

"No, thank you, Uncle Andy," replied the Babe politely.

"But you haven't asked a single question for at least seven minutes," said Uncle Andy.

"I was too busy listening to you," explained the Babe. "But there's one I'd like to ask, if it's all the same to you."

"Well, fire away," said his uncle.

"*Why* did they all fly away like that, as if they had just remembered something awfully important? And why would you rather be a little tiny humming-bird than a crow? And why did it take the whole flock that way to teach the young ones to fly? And—and why are they afraid, when they are *born* to fly? And why do they make fun of the stupid ones? And why would you like to be a wild goose? And, and——"

"Stop! stop!" cried Uncle Andy. "I didn't know you had a Gatling about you when I told you to fire away. You wait and shoot those questions at Bill, just like that, to-night."

"Well, but why——"

"No, you must not interrupt," insisted Uncle Andy.

"But you *asked* me! I was just as quiet ——"

"I didn't know what I was doing!" said his uncle. "And I can't possibly answer all those questions. Why, I could never begin to remember half of them."

"I can," interposed the Babe.

"Oh, you needn't mind," said Uncle Andy,

hastily. "But perhaps, if you listen with great care, you *may* find answers to some of them in what I am going to tell you. Of course, I don't promise, for I don't know what you asked me. But *maybe* you'll hear something that will throw some light on the subject."

"Thank you very much," said the Babe.

"There were only two young ones in the nest," said Uncle Andy, in his sometimes irrelevant way, which seemed deliberately designed to make the Babe ask questions. "The nest was a big, untidy structure of sticks and dead branches; but it was strongly woven for all its untidiness, because it had to stand against the great winds sweeping down over the Ridge. Inside it was very nicely and softly lined with dry grass, and some horsehair, and a piece of yellow silk from the lining of what had once been a ruffle or something like that that women wear. The nest was in a tall pine, which stood at one end of a grove of ancient fir trees overlooking a slope of pasture and an old white farmhouse with a big garden behind it. Nearly all the trees had crows' nests in their tops, but in most of the other nests there were three or four young crows."

As Uncle Andy paused again at this point the Babe, who was always polite, felt that he was really expected to ask a question here. If he did not, it might look as if he were not taking an interest. He would rather ask too many questions than run the risk of seeming inappreciative.

"*Why* were there only two young ones in the nest in the pine tree?" he inquired.

It was very hard to know sometimes just what would please Uncle Andy, and what wouldn't. But this time it was quite all right.

"Now, that's a proper, sensible question," said he. "I was just coming to that. You see, there ought to have been four youngsters in that nest, too, for there had been four greeny-blue, brown-spotted eggs to start with. But even crows have their troubles. And the pair that owned this particular nest were a somewhat original and erratic couple. When the mother had laid her last egg and was getting ready to sit, she decided to take an airing before settling down to work. Though her mate was not at hand to guard the nest, she flew off down to the farm to see if there was anything new going on among those foolish men, or perhaps to catch a mouse among the cornstalks."

"Do *crows* eat *mice?*" demanded the Babe in astonishment.

"Of course they do," answered Uncle Andy impatiently. "Everybody that eats meat at all eats mice, except us human beings. And in some parts of the world we, too, eat them, dipped in honey."

"Oh—h—h!" shuddered the Babe.

"Well, as I was going to say when you interrupted me, no sooner was she well out of the way than a red squirrel, who had been watching from the nearest fir tree, saw his chance. It was a rare one. Nobody liked eggs better than he did, or got fewer of them. Like a flash he was over from the fir branches into the pine ones, and up and into the nest.

"His sharp teeth went into the nearest egg, and he drank its contents greedily—and cleverly, let me tell you, for it's not so easy to manage without getting it all over your fur. He was just going to begin on another when there was a sharp hiss of wings just above him and a loud *ca-ah* of alarm. The father bird was back and swooping down upon him.

He threw himself clear of the nest, fell to a lower branch, and raced out to its tip to spring into his fir tree. At this moment the furious father struck him, knocking him clean off into the air.

"The air was now full of black wings and angry cries, as the crows from neighboring nests flocked to the help of their fellow citizen. But the little red robber was brave and kept his head. Spreading his legs wide and flat, he made a sort of parachute of himself, and, instead of falling like a stone, he glided down to another branch. Those beating wings and terrible jabbing beaks were all about him, but they got in each other's way. And he was a wonder at dodging, I can tell you, now that he was among the bigger branches, and, though he got several nasty thrusts, which covered his fine coat with blood, he gained his hole, halfway down the tree, and whisked into it safely.

"Into this narrow retreat, of course, none of the crows dared to follow him, knowing that they would there be at the mercy of his teeth. But they gathered in fierce excitement about the entrance, scolding the audacious thief at the top of their voices, and threatening him with every kind of vengeance when he should dare to come out. And from time to time one or another of the boldest would alight on the very edge of the hole, cock his head, and peer in, to bounce away again instantly with a startled squawk as the squirrel would jump up at him, chattering with rage.

"In the midst of all this excitement the careless mother came hurrying back. She had heard the row, of course. One could hear it all over the parish. Unobserved, she flew straight to the nest. Her big, dark, cunning eyes blazed for an instant, but she knew it was all her fault, and she thought it best to make no fuss. Hastily she dropped the empty shell over the side of the nest, and then took her place dutifully on the three remaining eggs. In a few minutes the rest of the crows got tired of scolding the squirrel in his hole and came *ca*-ing back to the pine tree to talk the matter over. When her mate, all in a fume, hopped onto the edge of the nest, the mother looked up at him with eyes of cold inquiry, as much as to say: 'Well, I'd like to know what all this fuss is about. You ought to be ashamed of yourself, acting that way about a wretched squirrel!' Of course, she may not have said all that. But she certainly gave all the other crows the impression that there was nothing wrong about *her* nest, and that they had better go and look after their own. Thereupon they all said sarcastic things to their fellow citizen and left him indignantly. He, poor fellow, found it imposible to explain or justify himself, because his mate was sitting on the eggs; so he flew off in a huff to try and find a sparrow's nest to rob. When he came back he had taken pains to forget just how many eggs there had ever been in the nest.

"Oh, yes, I know there were still three. Well, three or four days later a boy came up from the farmhouse and climbed the pine tree. He was not the kind of a boy that robs birds' nests, but he was making a collection. He wanted just one crow's egg, and he had a theory that birds cannot count. He liked crows—in fact, on that farm no one was ever allowed to shoot crows or any other birds except the murderous duck hawk, and he felt that the crows owed him *one* egg, anyhow, in return for the protection they enjoyed on his father's property.

"Now, you must not think he chose the pine tree because it was the easiest to climb," went on Uncle Andy hurriedly, seeing in the Babe's eyes that this point had to be cleared up at once. "In fact, it was the *hardest* to climb. Any one of the fir trees would have been easier, and they all had crows' nests in them. But the boy knew that he could not climb any of them without getting his clothes all over balsam, which would mean a lot of inconvenient explanations with his mother. So he went up the pine tree, of course, and spared his mother's feelings.

"The crows displayed no sense of gratitude whatever. He might have eggs, of course, that boy, but not *their* eggs! They flapped around him savagely, and made so much noise in his ears that he could not hear himself think. But he kept his big straw hat pulled down well over his eyes, and paid no attention whatever to the indignant birds. And because he was so quiet and positive about it, not one of them *quite* dared to actually touch him. The mother bird hopped off the nest sullenly just as he was about to put his hand on her. He took one egg, put it in his pocket, examined the nest with interest, and climbed down again. Just as he was nearing the ground he broke the egg. This, of course, made him feel not only sticky but somewhat embarrassed. He saw that he might have some difficulty in explaining that pocket to his mother. Even a great deal of balsam would have been better than *that* egg. But he comforted himself with the thought that he would never have been able to blow it, anyhow, on account of its being so advanced.

"And that's why there were only two young crows in that particular nest.

"But they were an altogether unusual pair, these two. In the first place, receiving all the food and all the attention that were usually divided among four or five, they had grown and feathered extraordinarily fast, till now they were ready for flight, while their fellows in the neighboring nests were still ragged and "quilly" looking. In the second place, they had inherited from their eccentric parents an altogether surprising amount of originality. Their feathers were beautifully firm and black and glossy, their beaks sharp and polished; and in their full, dark, intelligent eyes there was an impishness that even a crow might regard as especially impish."

"What's *impish?*" demanded the Babe.

"Goodness me! Don't you know what *impish* is?" exclaimed Uncle Andy. He thought a moment, and then, finding it a little difficult to explain, he added with convenient severity: "If you will listen, you'll find out, perhaps."

"Well, the two grew so fast that, before their parents realized at all what precocious youngsters they were, they had climbed out upon the edge of the nest and begun to stretch their fine wings. With hoarse expostulations their father tried to persuade them back. But their mother, who was not so conservative, chuckled her approval and flew off to hunt young mice for them. Thus encouraged, they ignored their father's prudent counsels, and hopped out, with elated squawks, upon the branch. Whereupon the father, somewhat huffed, flew up to the very topmost branch of the tree and perched there, swaying in the breeze, and trying to forget his family cares. From this high post of observation he presently caught sight of an eagle, winging his way up from the swamp at the lower end of the valley. With a sharp signal cry for volunteers, he dashed off in pursuit. He was joined by two other crows who happened to be at leisure; and the three, quickly overtaking the majestic voyager, began to load him with impertinence and abuse. With their comparatively short but very broad wings the crows could dodge so nimbly in the air that it was quite impossible for their great enemy to catch them. He made no attempt to do so. Indignantly he changed the direction of his flight, and began to soar, climbing gradually into the blue in splendid, sweeping circles; while the crows, croaking mockery and triumph, kept flapping above him and below, darting at his eyes, and dashing with open beaks at the shining whiteness of his crown. They dared not come near enough to actually touch him, but they succeeded in making themselves most unpleasant. The eagle glared at them steadily with his fierce, black-and-yellow eyes, but otherwise seemed to pay them no attention whatever. Only he kept mounting higher and higher, till at last his impish tormentors

—*impish,* I said—dared follow him no farther. They came fluttering down hurriedly to more congenial levels, and flew back to the grove to boast of their 'great victory.' "

"My, but that eagle must have felt awfully ashamed!" exclaimed the Babe.

"The *next* day," continued Uncle Andy, without noticing the interruption, "the two old crows began to think it would soon be time to teach this independent pair of youngsters to fly. And they thought, too, that they'd be able to manage it all by themselves, without any help or advice from the rest of the flock. While they were thinking about it, in the next tree, for they were not a great pair to stay at home, you know, one of the youngsters, the female, gave an impatient squawk, spread her wings, and fell off her branch. She thought it was flying, you know, but at first she just fell, flapping her wings wildly. In two seconds, however, she seemed to get the hang of it, more or less. With a violent effort, she rose, gained the next tree, alighted, panting, beside her parents and looked at them with a superior air, as if she thought that they could never have accomplished such a thing at her age.

That was perhaps true, of course, but it was not for her to think so."

"Huh! I should think not, indeed!" agreed the Babe severely.

"Well," continued Uncle Andy, now quite absorbed in his narrative, "the other youngster, not to be outdone, went hopping up in great excitement from branch to branch, till he was some ten feet above the rest of the family. Then, launching himself boldly, he went fluttering down to them with no difficulty at all. He was less impetuous and more sagacious than his sister.

"After this the parents continued to feed their independent offspring for a number of days, just because they had been accustomed to feed their nestling for a certain length of time, till at last the youngsters started off to forage on their own account, and the family, as a family, broke up. From habit, however, or from good will, the youngsters kept coming back to roost on the branches beside the nest, and remained on the most friendly, though easy-going, relations with their father and mother.

"In every crow flock, large or small, there

seems to be some kind of discipline, some kind of obedience to the wise old leaders of the flock. But the two black imps of Pine-Top were apparently, for the time at least, exempted from it. They did about as they liked and were a nuisance to everybody but their two selves, whom they admired immensely. Being too young for the old crows to take seriously, their pranks were tolerated, or they would soon have been pecked and beaten into better manners. Too big and too grown-up for the young crows—whom they visited in their nests and tormented till driven away by the indignant parents—they had no associates but each other. So they followed their own whims; and the flock was philosophically indifferent as to what might happen to them.

"You must not think, however, that they did not learn anything, these two. They were sharp. They listened to what was being said around them, and the crows, you know, are the greatest talkers ever; so they soon knew the difference betwen a man with a gun and a man without one. They knew that an owl in the daytime is not the same thing as an owl at night. They gathered that a scarecrow is not as dangerous as it looks. And many other things that a crow needs to know and believe they condescended to learn, because learning came easy to them. But common caution they did not learn, because it did not seem to them either interesting or necessary. So it was often just luck that got them out of scrapes, though they always thought it was their own cleverness.

"It was just lucky, of course, that day when they went exploring in the patch of dark woods down in the valley, that the big brown owl did not get one or the other of them. He was asleep on a big dead branch as brown as himself, and looking so like a part of it that they were just going to alight, either upon him or within reach of his deadly clutch, when a red squirrel saw them and shrieked at them. Two great, round, glaring orange eyes opened upon them from that brown prong of the branch, so suddenly that they gave two startled squawks and nearly fell to the ground. How the red squirrel tittered, hating both the owl and the crows. But the imps, when they got over their start, were furious. Flying over the owl's head, they kept screaming at the top of their voices something which probably meant 'an owl! an owl! an owl!'; and immediately every other crow within hearing took up the cry, till in two minutes half the flock were gathered in the patch of woods. They swarmed screaming about the owl's head, striking at him with their sharp beaks and strong black wings, but always to wary to come quite within his reach. The great night prowler knew that in the daylight he could not catch them—that, indeed, if he did succeed in catching one in his claws the others would throw caution to the winds and all be down upon him at once. He sat there, straight and stiff, for a while, snapping his terrible beak and hissing at them like an angry cat. Till at last, realizing that there was no more chance of a peaceful sleep for him there, he spread his huge, downy wings and sailed off smoothly to seek some more secluded neighborhood. The whole flock pursued him, with their tormenting and abuse, for perhaps a couple of miles; and then, at some signal from their leaders, dropped the chase suddenly and turned their attention to what looked like a sort of game of tag, in a wide, open pasture where no enemy could steal upon them unawares. The imps felt themselves great heroes, but if it had not been for that red squirrel, the owl, sleepy though he was, would certainly have got one of them."

The Babe wanted to ask whether the squirrel had warned them out of friendliness or just out of dislike to the owl, but before he could frame his question quite satisfactorily, or get out anything more than a hasty "But why——?" Uncle Andy had gone on with an emphasis which discouraged interruption.

"It was lucky for them, too, that no guns were fired on the big farm below the grove—the crows were there believed to earn the corn they stole by the grubs and cutworms and mice they killed. That was *very* lucky for the two imps, for they were forever hanging about the farmyard and the big locust trees that ran along the foot of the garden. The farmer himself and his hired hands paid no attention to them, but the boy, the one who had prevented there being three imps instead of two, he was tremendously interested. At first they were shy of him, because, perhaps, they felt him watching them out of the corners of his keen blue eyes. But at last they decided he was no more dangerous than the rest, and made sarcastic remarks about him in a language which he couldn't understand.

"There was always food to be picked up around the farmyard when the men were absent in the fields, the womenfolk busy in the kitchen, and the boy somewhere out of sight. And it was food doubly sweet because it had to be stolen from the fussy hens or the ridiculous ducks or the stupid, complacent pigeons. Then there was always something interesting to be done. It was fun to bully the pigeons and to give sly, savage jabs to the half-grown chicks. It was delightful to steal the bright tops of tin tomato cans—they *thought* they were stealing them, of course, because they could not imagine such fascinating things being thrown away, even by those fool men—to snatch them hurriedly, fly off with them to the tall green pine-top, and hide them in their old nest till they got it looking quite like a rubbish dump, and good pasture for a goat. And most of all, perhaps, was it fun to tease the lazy old kitchen cat, till her tail would get as big as a bottle brush with helpless indignation."

"The *cat?*" exclaimed the Babe. "Why, weren't they afraid of *her?*"

"Wait and see!" remarked Uncle Andy simply, with no apologies whatever to the Prime Minister. "Well, as I was about to say, their method was simple and effective. They would wait till they found the cat lying along the narrow top of the rail fence, sunning herself. It was her favorite place, though it can hardly have been comfortable, it was so narrow. The He imp would alight on the rail, about ten feet in front of her, and pretend to be very sick, squawking feebly and drooping his black wings with a struggling flutter, as if it was all he could do to keep his perch. The cat, her narrow eyes opening very wide, would start to creep up to him. The She imp would then alight on the rail behind her and nip her sharply by the tail, and go hopping clumsily off down the rail. The cat would wheel with an angry *pfiff-ff*, and start after this new quarry. Whereupon the He imp would again nip her tail. This would be repeated several times before the cat would realize that she was being made a fool of. Then she would bounce down from the fence and race off to the kitchen in a towering rage, and the impudent youngsters would fly up into the nearest tree top and *ca* about it delightedly.

"Then there was the scarecrow, in the middle of the big strawberry patch down at the foot of the huge garden. It did not scarce these two young rascals, not in the least. It was an excellently made scarecrow, and did strike terror to the heart of many of the smaller birds. But its hat was packed with straw, and the imps found it was a pleasant game pulling the straws out through a couple of holes in the crown, and strewing them over the strawberry bed. Incidentally, they liked strawberries, and ate a good many of them as sauce to their ordinary diet of grubs and mice and chicken feed. And it was this weakness of theirs for strawberries that led to their misunderstanding with the Boy, and then with the big rat that lived under the tool shed.

"That strawberry patch was one of the things that the Boy took a particular interest in. When he saw that the imps also took such an interest in it, eating the berries instead of the grubs, he began to get annoyed. From his window, which overlooked the garden, he had seen what liberties the imps took with the scarecrow, so he realized there was no help for him in scarecrows. But *something* must be done, that he vowed, and done at once, or his strawberries were going to be mighty scarce. He didn't want to do any real harm to even such a troublesome pair of birds as the imps, but he was determined to give them a lesson that might teach them some respect, not only for strawberry patches, but even for scarecrows.

"On the crown of the scarecrow's old hat, which he had observed to be a favorite perch of the imps, he arranged a noose of light cord. From the noose he ran the cord down the scarecrow's single leg (scarecrows, you know, have usually only one leg), across to the hedge, along the hedge to the house, and up and into his room. He fixed it so it ran without a hitch. He was very proud of it altogether. Much pleased with himself, he got a book and a couple of apples, and seated himself at his window to wait for his chance.

"As it happened, however, the imps were just then away in the meadow, hunting mice. For a whole hour the Boy saw no sign of them. Then, being called away to go on an errand into the village, he tied the end of the cord to his bedpost, and left it with a word of advice to do what it could in his absence.

"Well, it did! For a mere bit of string, all by itself, it didn't do badly. First the old brown rat, with his fierce little eyes and pointed, whiskered nose, came out from under the toolhouse and began exploring the strawberry patch. He didn't think much of strawberries in themselves, but he was apt to find fat grubs and beetles and sleepy June bugs under the clustering leaves. He came upon the string, stretched taut. He was just about to bite it through and try to carry it off to his nest when it occurred to him it might be a trap. He turned away discreetly, and snapped up a plump June bug.

"Then the imps came sailing along. The He imp, with a loud *ca-ah,* perched in the top of a locust and reconnoitred the situation. The She imp alighted on the head of the scarecrow, cocked her head to one side, and peered down upon the rat with a wicked and insulting eye. *'Cr-r-r-r,'* she said sarcastically. But, as the rat paid no attention to her, she hopped up and down on her toes, half-lifting her wings in the effort to attract his eye. She hated to be ignored. But still the rat ignored her, though he saw her perfectly well and would have loved to eat her. At last, in her excitement, she caught sight of the cord running over the edge of the scarecrow's hat. Snatching it up in her beak, she gave it an energetic and inquiring tug. She learned something interesting about it at once. It grabbed her by one leg.

"Startled into a panic, as all wild things are at the least suggestion of restraint, she squawked and flapped into the air. The noose tightened rebukingly and pulled her up short.

"For one astounded moment she settled back onto the scarecrow's head, frightened into stillness. Then she tweaked savagely at the cord on her leg, but, of course, could do nothing with it. As far as knots were concerned, her education had been utterly neglected. At last she sprang once more into the air, determined to have nothing more to do with the treacherous scarecrow who had stuck that thing on her leg.

"Of course, she didn't fly far—just about

six feet—and she was again brought up with a jerk. And now she went quite wild. Squawking and flapping and whirling round and round, she made an amazing exhibition of herself. Her brother, in the top of the locust, stared down upon her in astonished disapproval. And the brown rat, interested at last, came creeping stealthily to the scarecrow's foot and looked up at her performance with cruel, glinting eyes.

"Now, as you may well imagine, this performance was something which even the imp, strong as she was, could not keep up very long. In about a minute she had to stop and take breath. She was going to alight on the ground, when she remembered the rat. Yes, there he was. So she had to take refuge once more on the hated and treacherous scarecrow. But no sooner had she done so, alighting with open beak and half-spread, quivering wings, than the rat came darting up the leg of the scarecrow's ragged trousers and pounced at her. She *just* escaped, and that was all, leaping into the air with a squawk of terror and flapping there violently at the end of those six feet of free cord.

"It was a horrifying position for her, let me tell you——"

"I guess *so!*" muttered the Babe in spite of himself, wagging his head sympathetically. He did not like rats.

"She was too frightened to save her strength, of course, and so kept flapping with all her might, as if she thought to fly away with scarecrow and all. The rat, however, was impatient. He clutched at the cord with his handlike claws and began trying to pull the imp down to him. At first he couldn't make much out of it, but as the imp weakened with her frantic efforts the cord began to shorten. Just about now the He imp, who had come down from the locust top and fluttered over the scene in pained curiosity, realized what was happening. He was game, all right, however bumptious and self-satisfied. He set up a tremendous *ca-a-a-ing,* as a signal for all the crows within hearing to come to the rescue, and then made a sudden, savage side swoop at the foe.

"Taken thoroughly by surprise, the rat was toppled from his unsteady perch and fell among the strawberries. His head ringing from the stroke of that sturdy black wing, his plump flank smarting and bleeding from a fierce jab of that pointed beak of the imp's, he squeaked with rage and clambered up again to the battle. Mr. Rat, you know, is no coward and no quitter.

"And now he was more dangerous, because he was ready. He sat warily on his haunches, squeaking angrily, and turning his sharp head from side to side as he followed every swoop and rush of the He imp, snapping so dangerously that the latter did not dare come quite close enough to deliver another really effective blow. At the same time, being very clever indeed, the rat kept tugging, tugging, tugging at the cord. And the She imp, being quite gone out of her mind with the terror of that clutch on her leg, kept flapping crazily at the end of the cord instead of turning to, like a sensible crow, and helping her brother in the fight.

"As she grew weaker and weaker in her struggles, the cunning rat drew her lower and lower, till at last she seemed fairly within his reach. He lifted himself on his hindquarters to snap his long teeth into her thigh and spring to the ground with her, where he would have her completely at his mercy. But as he rose the He imp, at sight of his sister's deadly peril, lost all sense of caution, and struck again with all his strength of beak and wing. And once more the rat, fairly bursting with rage, was swept to the ground.

"He was back to the attack again in a moment, and now more dangerous than ever. And at the same time the She imp, utterly worn out at last by her panic terror and her foolish violence, sank shuddering down upon her perch. Her brother struck the rat again frantically when the latter was halfway up the scarecrow's leg, but this time failed to dislodge him. And it looked as if the poor She imp would never again steal a strawberry or worry a pigeon. But at this moment the Boy appeared in the garden. He came running up noiselessly, anxious to see all that was happening. But the rat heard him. The rat had no use for the Boy whatever. He knew that the whole human race was his enemy. He dropped from the scarecrow's trouser leg and scurried off to his hole beneath the toolhouse. The Boy, his face a mixture of amusement and concern, picked up the captive without noticing her feeble pecks, undid the noose from her leg, and carried her over the hedge to rest and recover herself.

"'Now,' said he, 'you little imp of Satan, maybe you'll not come stealing any more of my strawberries or pulling any more straw out of my poor scarecrow's head!'

"And she never did!" concluded Uncle Andy, rising and stretching his legs. "Those two were not *reformed,* you may be sure. But they kept clear, after that, of the Boy's strawberry patch, and of *all scarecrows.* It's time we were getting back to camp for supper, or Bill will be feeling sour."

"But you haven't told me," protested the Babe, who had a most tenacious memory, "why those crows all flew away out of the pine-top so suddenly, as if they had just remembered something. And you haven't told me why you'd rather be a humming-bird than a crow. And you haven't——"

But Uncle Andy stopped him.

"If you think I'm going to tell you all I know," said he, "you're mistaken. If I did, you'd know as much as I do, and it wouldn't be any fun. Some day you'll be glad I've left something for you to find out for yourself."

CHAPTER III

YOUNG GRUMPY AND THE ONE-EYED GANDER

"My gracious! What's that?" cried the Babe, and nearly jumped out of his boots. A gray thing had come right at him, with an ugly, scurrying rush. The bushes and bracken being thick, he had not got a very clear view of it—and he did not stop to try for a better one. In two seconds he was back at Uncle Andy's side, where the latter sat smoking on his favorite log by the water.

The Babe's eyes were very wide. He looked a bit startled.

"It ran *straight* at me!" he declared. "What could it have been?"

"A bear, I suppose!" said Uncle Andy sarcastically.

"Of course not," answered the Babe in an injured voice. "If it had been a bear, I'd have been *frightened*."

"Oh!" said Uncle Andy. "I see. Well,

what was it like? Seems to me you didn't take much time to look at it, even if you *weren't* frightened."

"I *did* look," protested the Babe, glancing again, a little nervously, at the bushes. "It was like—like a tre-*mendous* big fat guinea pig, with a fat tail and all kind of rusty gray."

"Now, that's not at all bad, considering you were in something of a hurry," said Uncle Andy approvingly. "That's really a very good description of a woodchuck. No one could possibly mistake it for a lobster or a lion."

"Of course, I couldn't see it very *plain,*" added the Babe hastily, wondering if Uncle Andy was laughing at him. "But why did it run at me that way?"

"You see," said Uncle Andy seriously, repenting of his mockery, "the woodchuck is a queer, bad-tempered chap, with more pluck than sense sometimes. Once in a while he would run at anything that was new and strange to him, no matter how big it was, just to see if he couldn't frighten it."

"Would he run at you or Bill that way?"

demanded the Babe in a voice of awe at the very thought of such temerity.

"Oh, he has seen lots of *men,*" replied Uncle Andy. "We're nothing new to him. But most likely he had never seen a small boy before, and he did not know what kind of an animal it was. The very fact that he did not know made him angry—he's sometimes so quick-tempered, you know!"

"I'm glad he didn't frighten me—so *very* much!" murmured the Babe, beginning to forget the exact degree of his alarm.

"I noticed you got out of his way pretty smart!" said Uncle Andy, eyeing him from under shaggy brows. "But perhaps that was just because you were in a hurry to tell me about it!"

"No-o!" answered the Babe, hesitating but truthful. "I thought perhaps he was going to bite my legs, and I didn't want him to."

"That seems reasonable enough," agreed Uncle Andy heartily. "No sensible person wants a fool woodchuck biting his legs."

"But would he *really* have bitten me?" asked the Babe, beginning to think that perhaps he ought to go back and find the presumptuous little animal and kick him.

"As I think I've already said, you never can tell exactly what a woodchuck is going to do," replied Uncle Andy. "You know that old rhyme about him:

'How much wood would a woodchuck chuck,
If a woodchuck could chuck wood?
He'd chuck as much wood as a woodchuck could
If a woodchuck could chuck wood.'

Now that goes to show what uncertainty people have about him. And it's no more than right. For instance, I was traveling through a wild part of New Brunswick once in a big red automobile, when, coming suddenly around a turn, we saw just ahead of us two old woodchucks sitting up on their fat haunches by the side of the road. I was beside the chauffeur, and could see just what happened. How those woodchucks' eyes stuck out! It was not more than three seconds before we were right up to them. Then one of the two, frightened to death, fairly turned a back somersault into the bushes. But the other was a hero. Perhaps he thought he was St. George and the automobile a dragon. Anyhow, he did all a hero could. He jumped straight on to the front wheel and bit wildly at the tire. We stopped so short that we almost went out on our heads —but too late! The wheel had gone clean over him. We felt so sorry that we stopped and dug a hole by the roadside and gave the flattened little hero a very distinguished burial."

"Oh, but he must have been crazy!" exclaimed the Babe, rubbing his leg thoughtfully and congratulating himself that he had not lingered to study the being which had rushed at him in the underbrush.

"Perhaps," said Uncle Andy dryly. "If I remember rightly, that's just what has been said of lots of heroes before now."

He tapped his pipe on the log beside him to knock out the ashes, and proceeded thoughtfully to fill it up again. This second filling the Babe had learned to regard as a very hopeful sign. It usually meant that Uncle Andy was in the vein. Seating himself on the grass directly in front of his uncle, the Babe clasped his arms around his bare little brown, mosquito-bitten knees, and stared upward hopefully with grave, round eyes, as blue as the bluebells nodding beside him.

"Speaking of woodchucks," began Uncle Andy presently, "I've known a lot of them in my time, and I've almost always found them interesting. Like some people we know, they're sometimes most amusing when they are most serious."

"Amusing!" exclaimed the Babe, with a world of meaning in his voice. That was the last word he expected to apply to such a bad-tempered little beast.

But his uncle paid no heed to the interruption.

"There was 'Young Grumpy,' now," he continued musingly. "As sober-minded a woodchuck as ever burrowed a bank. From his earliest days he took life seriously, and never seemed to think it worth his while to play as the other wild youngsters do. Yet in spite of himself he was sometimes quite amusing.

"He had the good fortune to be born in the back pasture of Anderson's Farm. That was where the Boy lived, you know, and where no one was allowed to shoot the crows. Being a place where no one did any more killing than was absolutely necessary, it was rather lucky for any of the Babes of the Wild to be born there—except weasels, of course."

"Why not for weasels?" demanded the Babe.

"Well, now, you might know that without my having to tell you," replied Uncle Andy. "The weasels are such merciless and murderous little killers themselves, killing just for the fun of it when they are already too full to eat what they have killed, that both Mr. Anderson and the Boy had no sympathy for them, and thought them better out of the way. I don't want to be too hard, even on a weasel; but I'm bound to say that most of the wild creatures feel much the same way about that bloodthirsty little pirate."

"I should think so!" agreed the Babe indignantly, resolving to devote his future largely to the extermination of weasels, and hoping thus to win the confidence and gratitude of the kindred of the wild.

"Young Grumpy's home life," continued Uncle Andy, "with his father and mother and four brothers and sisters was not a pampered one. There are few wild parents less given to spoiling their young than a pair of grumbling old woodchucks. The father, who spent most of his time sleeping, rolled up in a ball at the bottom of the burrow, paid them no attention except to nip at them crossly when they tumbled over him. They were always relieved when he went off, three or four times a day, down into the neighboring clover field to make his meals. The little ones did not see what he was good for, anyhow, till one morning, when the black-and-yellow dog from the next farm happened along. The youngsters, with their mother, were basking in the sun just outside the front door. As the dog sprang at them they all fairly fell, head over heels, back into the burrow. The dog, immensely disappointed, set to work frantically to dig them out. He felt sure that young woodchuck would be very good to eat.

"It was then that Old Grumpy showed what he was made of. Thrusting his family rudely aside, he scurried up the burrow to the door, where the dog was making the earth fly at a most alarming rate. Without a moment's hesitation he sank his long, cutting teeth into the rash intruder's nose and held on.

"The dog yelped and choked, and tried to back out of the hole in a hurry. But it was no use. The old woodchuck had a solid grip and was pulling with all his might in the other direction. Panic-stricken and half smothered by the dry earth, the dog dug in his hind claws, bent his back like a bow, and pulled for all he was worth, yelling till you might have thought there were half a dozen dogs in that hole. At last, after perhaps three or four minutes—which seemed to the dog much longer—the old woodchuck decided to leave go. You see, he didn't really want that dog, or even that dog's nose, in the burrow. So he opened his jaws suddenly. At that the dog went right over backward, all four legs in the air, like a wooden dog. But the next instant he was on his feet again, and tearing away like mad down the pasture, ki-yi-ing like a whipped puppy, although he was a grown-up dog and ought to have been ashamed of himself to make such a noise. And never after that, they tell me, could he be persuaded under any circumstances to go within fifteen feet of anything that looked like a woodchuck hole."

"I'm not one bit sorry for him," muttered

"He was a grown-up dog and ought to have been ashamed of hmself."

the Babe in spite of himself. "He had no business there at all."

"The mother of the woodchuck family," went on Uncle Andy, "was not so cross as the father, but she was very careless. She would sit upon her fat haunches in the door of the burrow while the babies were nibbling around outside, pretending to keep an eye on them. But half the time she would be sound asleep, with her head dropped straight down on her stomach, between her little black paws. One day, as she was dozing thus comfortably, a marsh hawk came flapping low overhead, and pounced on one of the youngsters before it had time to more than squeak. At the sound of that despairing squeak, to be sure, she woke up and made a savage rush at the enemy. But the wary bird was already in the air, with the prize drooping from his talons. And the mother could do nothing but sit up and chatter after him abusively as he sailed away to his nest.

"You see, the mother was brave enough, as I said before, but very careless. She was different from the ordinary run of woodchucks, in that she had only three feet. She had lost her left hind paw."

"Was that because she was so careless?" asked the Babe.

Uncle Andy looked at him suspiciously. Like so many other story-tellers, he preferred to make all the jokes himself. He was suspicious of other people's jokes. But the Babe's round, attentive eyes were as innocent as the sky.

"No," said he gravely; "*that* was something she could not help. It was an accident. It has nothing to do with Young Grumpy, but since you've asked me about it I had better tell you at once and save interruptions.

"You see it was this way. Before she came to live on the Anderson Farm she used to have a burrow over on the other side of the Ridge, where the people went in for a good deal of trapping and snaring. One day someone set a steel trap just in front of her burrow. Of course she put her foot into it at the first chance. It was terrible. You know the grip of those steel jaws, for I've seen you trying to open them. She was game, however—they're always game, these woodchucks. Instead of squealing and hopping about and losing her wits and using up her strength, she just popped back into her hole and dragged the trap in with her as far as it would go. That was not very far, of course, because the man who set it had chained it to a stump outside. But she thought it better, in such a trouble, to be out of range of unsympathetic eyes. There in the hole she tugged and wrenched at the cruel biting thing till even *her* obstinacy had to acknowledge that it was impossible to pull herself free. Then she tried blocking up the hole behind her, thinking perhaps that the trap, on finding itself thus imprisoned in the burrow, would get frightened and let go its hold. Disappointed in this hope, she decided to adopt heroic measures. With magnificent nerve she calmly set to work and *gnawed off* the foot which had been so idiotic as to get itself caught. She would have nothing more to do with the fool thing. She just left it there in the trap, with her compliments, for the man—a poor little, crumpled, black-skinned paw, with a fringe of short brownish fur about the wrist, like a fur-lined gauntlet."

The Babe shuddered, but heroically refrained from interrupting.

"Of course the stump soon healed up," continued Uncle Andy, "but she always found the absence of that paw most inconvenient, especially when she was digging burrows. She used to find herself digging them on the bias, and coming out where she did not at all expect to.

"But to return to Young Grumpy. While he was yet very young his three-legged mother, who had seen him and his brothers and sisters eating grass quite comfortably, decided that they were big enough to look out for themselves. She refused to nurse them any more. Then she turned them all out of the burrow. When they came presently scurrying back again, hoping it was all an unhappy joke, she nipped them most unfeelingly. Their father snored. There was no help in that quarter. They scurried dejectedly forth again.

"Outside, in the short pasture grass and scattered ox-eye daisies, they looked at each other suspiciously, and each felt that somehow it was the other fellow's fault. Aggrieved and miserable, they went rambling off, each his own way, to face alone what Fate might have in store for him. And Young Grumpy, looking up from a melancholy but consoling feast which he was making on a mushroom, found himself alone in the world.

"He didn't care a fig. You see, he was so grumpy. Not knowing where to go, he strolled up the hill and into the fir woods. Here he came upon a very old, moth-eaten, feeble-looking woodchuck, who was very busy in a half-hearted way digging himself a hole. Suddenly he stopped. Young Grumpy did not think it was any sort of a hole for a woodchuck, but the old fellow seemed satisfied with it. He curled himself up in it, almost in plain view, and went straight to sleep. Young Grumpy strolled off scornfully. When he came back that way, a few hours later, he found the old woodchuck still in exactly the same position as before. He never stirred or scolded even when Young Grumpy came up and squeaked quite close to his ear. Seized suddenly with a vague uneasiness, Young Grumpy nosed at him curiously. The old woodchuck's body was chill and rigid. It created a most unpleasant impression, and, not knowing why he did so, Young Grumpy hurried forth from the dark wood and down into the sunlit pasture to which he was accustomed.

"For some days he wandered about the pasture, sleeping under stumps and in mossy hollows, and fortunately escaping, by reason of his light, rusty-gray color, the eyes of passing hawks. At last chance, or his nose for good living, led him down to the clover meadow adjoining Anderson's barnyard.

"It was here that his adventures may be said to have begun.

"Just as he was happily filling himself with clover, a white dog, with short-cropped ears standing up stiffly, came by and stopped to look at him with bright, interested eyes. Young Grumpy, though the stranger was big enough to take him in two mouthfuls, felt not frightened but annoyed. He gave a chuckling squeak of defiance and rushed straight at the dog.

"Now, this was the Boy's bull terrier, Major, and he had been severely trained to let small, helpless creatures alone. He had got it into his head that all such creatures were the Boy's property, and so to be guarded and respected.

He was afraid lest he might hurt this cross little animal, and get into trouble with the Boy. So he kept jumping out of the way, stiff-leggedly, as if very much amused, and at the same time he kept barking, as if to call the Boy to come and see. Young Grumpy, feeling very big, followed him up with short, threatening rushes, till he found himself just at the open gate leading into the farmyard.

"Parading solemnly before the gate was a big gray gander with only one eye. That one eye, extra keen and fierce, caught sight of Young Grumpy, and probably mistook him for an immense rat, thief of eggs and murderer of goslings. With a harsh hiss and neck outstretched till it was like a snake, the great bird darted at him.

"Young Grumpy hesitated. After the manner of his kind, he sat upon his haunches to hesitate. The gander seemed to him very queer, and perhaps dangerous.

"At this critical moment the white dog interfered. In his eyes Young Grumpy belonged to the Boy, and was therefore valuable property. He ran at the gander. The gander, recognizing his authority, withdrew, haughty and protesting. Young Grumpy followed with a triumphant rush, and, of course, took all the credit to himself.

"This led him into the farmyard. Here he promptly forgot both the dog and the gander. It was such a strange place, and full of such strange smells. He was about to turn back into the more familiar clover when, as luck would have it, he stumbled upon a half-eaten carrot which had been dropped by one of the horses. How good it smelled! And then, how good it tasted! Oh, no! the place where such things were to be found was not a place for him to leave in a hurry!

"As he was feasting greedily on the carrot the Boy appeared, with the white dog at his heels. He did not look nearly so terrible as the gander. So, angry at being disturbed, and thinking he had come for the carrot, Young Grumpy ran at him at once.

"But the Boy did not run away. Surprised at his courage, Young Grumpy stopped short, at a distance of two or three feet from the Boy's stout shoes, sat upon his haunches with his little skinny black hands over his chest, and began to gurgle and squeak harsh threats.

The Boy laughed, and stretched out a hand to touch him. Young Grumpy snapped so savagely, however, that the Boy snatched back his hand and stood observing him with amused interest, waving off the white dog lest the latter should interrupt. Young Grumpy went on blustering with his muffled squeaks for perhaps a minute. Then, seeing that the Boy was neither going to run away nor fight, he dropped on all fours indifferently and returned to his carrot.

"There was nothing pleased the Boy better than seeing the harmless wild creatures get familiar about the place. He went now and fetched a saucer of milk from the dairy, and set it down beside Young Grumpy, who scolded at him, but refused to budge an inch. The yellow cat—an amiable soul, too well fed to hunt even mice with any enthusiasm—followed the Boy, with an interested eye on the saucer. At sight of Young Grumpy her back went up, her tail grew big as a bottle, and she spat disapprovingly. As the stranger paid her no attention, however, she sidled cautiously up to the milk and began to lap it.

"The sound of her lapping caught Young

Grumpy's attention. It was a seductive sound. Leaving the remains of his carrot, he came boldly up to the saucer. The yellow cat flattened back her ears, growled, and stood her ground till he was within a foot of her. Then, with an angry *'pf-f-f'* she turned tail and fled. The stranger was so calmly sure of himself that she concluded he must be some new kind of skunk—and her respect for all skunks was something tremendous.

"Having finished the milk and the carrot, Young Grumpy felt a pressing need of sleep. Turning his back on the Boy and the dog as if they were not worth noticing, he ambled off along the garden fence, looking for a convenient hole. The one-eyed gander, who had been watching him with disfavor from the distance, saw that he was now no longer under the protection of the white dog, and came stalking up from the other end of the yard to have it out with him—thief of eggs and murderer of goslings as the bird mistook him to be! But Young Grumpy, having found a cool-looking hole under the fence, had whisked into it and vanished.

"As matters stood now, Young Grumpy felt

himself quite master of the situation. His heartless mother was forgotten. Farmyard, clover-field, and cool green garden were all his. Had he not routed all presumptuous enemies but the Boy? And the latter seemed very harmless. But a few days the garden occupied all his attention—when he was not busy enlarging and deepening his hole under the fence and digging a second entrance to it. He noticed that the Boy had a foolish habit of standing and watching him; but to this he had no serious objection, the more so as he found that the Boy's presence was often accompanied by a saucer of milk.

"It was not till after several days of garden life that, lured by the memory of the carrot, he again visited the barnyard. At first it seemed to be quite deserted. And there was no sign of a carrot anywhere. Then he caught sight of the yellow cat, and scurried toward her, thinking perhaps it was her fault there were no carrots. She fluffed her tail, gave a yowl of indignation, and raced into the barn. Neither the white dog, nor the Boy, nor the one-eyed gander was anywhere in sight.

"Young Grumpy decided that it was a poor

place, the barnyard. He was on the point of turning back to the green abundance of the garden, when a curious clucking sound attracted his attention. At the other side of the yard he saw a red hen in a coop. A lot of very young chickens, little yellow balls of down, were running about outside the coop. Young Grumpy strolled over. The chickens did not concern him in the least. He didn't know what they were, and, as no flesh was in his eyes good to eat, he didn't care. But he hoped they might have such a thing as a carrot about them."

"Oh-h-h! What would *they* have a carrot for?" protested the Babe.

Uncle Andy scorned to notice this remark. "When Young Grumpy approached the coop," he continued, "the red hen squawked frantically, and the chickens all ran in under her wings. Young Grumpy eyed her with curiosity for a moment, as she screamed at him with open beak and ruffled up all her feathers. But in the coop was a big slice of turnip, at which she had been pecking. He knew at once this would be good, perhaps as good as a carrot, and he flattened himself against the bars trying to get in at it.

"The next moment he got a great surprise. The red hen hurled herself at him with such violence that, although the bars protected him, he was almost knocked over. He received a smart jab from her beak, and her bristling feathers came through the bars in a fashion that rather took away his breath. He was furious. Again and again he strove to force his way in, now on one side, now on the other. But always that fiery bunch of beak and claw and feathers seemed to burst in his face. Had it not been for the bars, indeed, the red hen would have given him an awful mauling. But this, of course, he was too self-confident to suspect. With characteristic obstinacy, he kept up the struggle for fully five minutes, while the terrified chickens filled the air with their pipings and the hen screamed herself hoarse. Then, feeling a little sore, to be sure, but very certain that he had impressed the hen, he strolled off to look for some delicacy less inaccessible than that piece of turnip.

"At this point the one-eyed gander came waddling up from the goose pond. He was lonely and bad-tempered, for his two wives had been killed by a fox that spring, and the Boy had not yet found him a new mate. Young Grumpy looked at the big gray bird and recalled the little unpleasantness of their previous encounter.

"'Oh, ho!' said he to himself—if woodchucks ever *do* talk to themselves—'I'll just give that ugly chap beans, like I did the other day.' And he went scurrying across the yard to see about it.

"To his surprise, the gander paid him no attention whatever. You see, he was on the side of the gander's blind eye.

"Now, Young Grumpy was so puzzled by this indifference that, instead of rushing right in and biting the haughty bird, he sat up on his haunches at a distance of some five or six feet and began to squeak his defiance. The gander turned his head. Straightway he opened his long yellow bill, gave vent to a hiss like the steam from an escape pipe, stuck out his snaky neck close to the ground, lifted his broad gray-and-white wings, and charged.

"Before Young Grumpy had time even to wonder if he had been imprudent or not, the

"Lifted his broad, gray-and-white wings, and charged."

hard elbow at one of those wings caught him a blow on the ear and knocked him head over heels [illegible] at the same [illegible] swept him to one side, and the gander landed [illegible] on the spot where he had been sitting.

Young Tommy picked himself up, startled and shaken. Then the [illegible] scared [illegible]. He would have rather liked to run away, but he was too [illegible] and [illegible]. He got up [illegible] his [illegible] determined to make another, and more successful attack as soon as his head stopped buzzing.

The gander, meanwhile, was surprised at [illegible]. He could not understand how his enemy had got out of the way so quickly. He hissed [illegible] and then, turning his [illegible] A [illegible] was [illegible] thought. Young [illegible] must have gone that way, he [illegible] a [illegible] [illegible] —and

The [illegible] strange [illegible] Young [illegible] for the [illegible] black [illegible] behind [illegible]. As [illegible] the gander saw him and swept [illegible] him [illegible]. But Young [illegible] his hard elbow of one of those wings caught him a blow on the ear and knocked him head over heels. At the same time it swept him to one side, and the gander rushed on straight over the spot where he had been sitting.

"Young Grumpy picked himself up, startled and shaken. The thing had been so unexpected. He would have rather liked to run away. But he was too angry and too obstinate. He just sat up on his haunches again, intending to make another and more successful attack as soon as his head stopped buzzing.

"The gander, meanwhile, was surprised also. He could not understand how his enemy had got out of the way so quickly. He stared around, and then, turning his one eye skyward, as if he thought Young Grumpy might have gone that way, he trumpeted a loud *honka-honka-honk—kah.*

"For some reason this strange cry broke Young Grumpy's nerve. He scuttled for his hole his jet-black heels kicking up the straws behind him. As soon as he began to run, of course, the gander saw him and swept after him with a ferocious hissing. But Young Grumpy had got the start. He dived into his hole just as the gander brought up against the fence.

"Now, the moment he found himself inside his burrow, all Young Grumpy's courage returned. He wheeled and stuck his head out again, as much as to say, '*Now* come on, if you dare!'

"The gander came on promptly—so promptly, in fact, that the lightning stroke of his heavy bill knocked Young Grumpy far back into the hole again.

"In a great rage, the gander darted his head into the hole. Chattering with indignation, Young Grumpy set his long teeth into that intruding bill, and tried to pull it further in. The gander, much taken aback at this turn of affairs, tried to pull it out again. For perhaps half a minute it was a very good tug-of-war. Then the superior weight and strength of the great bird, with all the advantage of his beating wings, suddenly triumphed, and Young Grumpy, too pig-headed to let go his hold, was jerked forth once more into the open.

"The next moment another blow from one of those mighty wing elbows all but stunned him, and his grip relaxed. He made a groping rush for the burrow, but in that same instant the gander's great bill seized him by the back of the neck and lifted him high into the air.

"This was very near being the end of Young Grumpy, for the one-eyed gander would have bitten and banged and hammered at him till he was as dead as a last year's June bug. But happily the Boy and the white dog came running up in the nick of time. The gander dropped his victim and stalked off haughtily. And poor Young Grumpy, after turning twice around in a confused way, crawled back into his hole.

"The white dog opened his mouth from ear to ear, and looked up at the Boy with an unmistakable grin. The Boy, half laughing, half sympathetic, went and peered into the hole.

" 'I guess you'd better keep out of Old Wall-Eye's way after this!' said he.

"And Young Grumpy did. Whenever the one-eyed gander was in the yard, then Young Grumpy stayed in the garden."

CHAPTER IV

LITTLE SWORD AND THE INKMAKER

Out across the shining expanse of Silverwater, now lying unruffled by any breath of wind, went flickering a little blue butterfly, as blue as if a gentian blossom had taken to itself wings or a speck of sky had fluttered down to meet its bright reflection in the lake. It was a foolish expedition for the little explorer, so far from shore, and over that lonely, treacherous element which has such scant mercy for butterflies. The turquoise wings dipped and rose, sometimes coming so close to the water that the Babe caught his breath, thinking the frail voyager's eyes were unable to distinguish between the crystal purity of the water and that of the air. At last a wing tip, or more likely the tip of the velvet tail, brushed the surface. It was only the lightest touch; and instantly, suddenly, as if startled by the chill contact, the azure flutterer rose again. In the same instant the water swirled heavily beneath her, a little sucking whirlpool appeared shattering the mirror, and circular ripples began to widen quickly and smoothly from the break.

"That was a big fellow!" exclaimed Uncle Andy. But the Babe said nothing, being too intent upon the aerial voyager's career.

For two or three moments the flake of sky fluttered higher. Then, as the ripples smoothed themselves out, she seemed to forget, and began to descend again as if lured downward by her own dainty reflection. Yet she had not quite forgotten, for now she only came within six or seven inches of the traitorous surface. Now her heavenly wings supported her for a moment almost motionless.

In that moment a splendid shape, gleaming like a bolt of silver, shot a clear foot into the air and fell back with a massive splash. The turquoise butterfly was gone.

"Oh—h!" cried the Babe, almost with a sob in his voice. He loved the blue butterflies as he loved no others of their brilliant and perishing kindred.

"Gee!" exclaimed Uncle Andy. "But he's a *whale!*"

The Babe, in his surprise at this remarkable statement, forgot to mourn for the fate of the blue butterfly.

"Why, Uncle Andy," he protested. "I didn't know whales could live here in this little lake."

Uncle Andy made a despairing gesture.

"Oh," he murmured wearily, "a fellow has to be *so* careful what he says to you! The next time I make a metaphorical remark in your presence, I'll draw a diagram to go with it!"

The Babe looked puzzled. He was on the point of asking what "a metaphorical" was, and also "a diagram"; but he inferred that there were no whales, after all, in Silverwater. He had misunderstood Uncle Andy's apparently simple statement of fact. And he felt convicted of foolishness. Anxious to reinstate himself in his uncle's approval by an unexpected display of knowledge he waived "metaphorical" aside, let "diagram" remain a mystery, and remarked disinterestedly:

"Well, I'm glad there ain't any *swordfish* in Silverwater."

"Bless the child!" cried Uncle Andy.

"Whatever has been putting swordfish into your head?"

"Bill!" replied the Babe truthfully.

"And what do you know about swordfish, then?" proceeded his uncle.

The Babe was much flattered at the unusual favor of being allowed to air his information.

"They're awful!" he explained. "They're as big as a canoe. And they've got a sword as long as your leg, Uncle Andy, right in their tail, so they can stab whales and porpoises with it, just carelessly, without looking round, so as to make pretend it was an accident. And they're quicker than greased lightning, Bill says. So you see, if there *was* one here in the lake, we couldn't ever go in swimming."

Uncle Andy refrained from smiling. He puffed thoughtfully at his pipe for half a minute, while the Babe waited for his verdict. At length he said, between puffs:

"Well, now, there's quite a lot of truth in that, considering that it's one of Bill's yarns. The swordfish *does* carry a sword. And he does jab it into things, whales, sharks, boats, seals, anything whatever that he thinks might be good to eat or that he does not like the looks of. And *you* are quite correct in thinking that the lake would not be a health-resort for us if it was occupied by a healthy swordfish. But in one particular Bill has got you badly mixed up. The swordfish carries his sword *not* in his tail, but on the tip of his snout more like a bayonet than a sword. I don't think Bill has ever been at all intimate with swordfish—eh, what?"

The Babe shook his blonde head sadly over this instance of Bill's inaccuracy.

"And are they as big as Bill says?" he inquired.

"Oh, yes! He's all right *there!*" assented Uncle Andy. "When they are quite grown up they are sometimes as long as a canoe, a seventeen or eighteen foot canoe. And they *are* quick as 'greased lightning' all right!"

"But how big are they when they're little?" pursued the Babe, getting around to his favorite line of investigation.

"Well now, that depends on how little you take them!" answered Uncle Andy. "As they are hatched out of tiny, pearly eggs no bigger than a white currant, which the little silver crabs can play marbles with on the white sand of the sea-bottom till they get tired of the game and eat them up, you've got a lot of sizes to choose from in a growing sword-fish."

"I don't mean when they're so *very* little," answered the Babe, who did not find things just hatched very interesting.

"I see," said Uncle Andy, understandingly. "Of course when they are first hatched, and for a long time afterwards, they are kept so busy trying to avoid getting eaten up by their enemies that I don't suppose one in ten thousand or so ever manages to survive to the stage where he begins to make things interesting for his enemies in turn. But *then* things begin to hum."

"Tell me how they hum!" said the Babe eagerly, his eyes round with anticipation.

"Well," began Uncle Andy slowly, looking far across the lake as if he saw things that the Babe could not see, "in one way and another, partly by good luck and partly by good management, Little Sword succeeded in dodging his enemies till he had grown to be about two feet in length, without counting the six inches or so of sharp, tapering blade that stood straight out from the tip of his nose. He was as handsome a youngster as you would wish to see, slender, gracefully tapering to the base of the broad, powerful tail, wide-finned, radiant in silver and blue-green, and with a splendid crestlike dorsal fin of vivid ultramarine extending almost the whole length of his back. His eyes were large, and blazed with a savage fire. Hanging poised a few feet above the tops of the waving, rose-and-purple sea-anemones and the bottle-green trailers of seaweed, every fin tense and quivering, he was ready to dart in any direction where a feast or a fight might seem to be waiting for him.

"You see, the mere fact that he was alive at all was proof that he had come triumphantly through many terrible dangers, so it was no wonder he had a good deal of confidence in himself. And his shapely little body was so packed full of energy, so thrilling with vitality, that he felt himself already a sort of lord in those shoal-water domains.

"But with all his lively experiences, there were things, lots of things, which Little Sword didn't know even yet."

"I *guess* so!" murmured the Babe, suddenly

impressed with the extent of his own ignorance

"For instance," Uncle Andy went on, ignoring the interruption, "he had not yet learned anything about the Inkmaker."

Here he paused impressively, as if to lure the Babe on. But into the latter's head popped so many questions all together, at the mention of a creature with so strange a name, that for the moment he could not for the life of him get any one of them into words. He merely gasped. And Uncle Andy, delighted with this apparent self-restraint, went on graciously.

"You're improving a lot," said he. "You're getting quite a knack of holding your tongue. Well, you're going to know all about it in half a minute.

"Little Sword caught sight of a queer, watery-pinkish, speckled creature on the bottom, just crossing a space of clear sand. It was about twice as long as himself, with a pair of terrible big, ink-black eyes, and a long bunch of squirming feelers growing out of its head like leaf-stalks out of the head of a beet. He noticed that two of these feelers were twice as long as the rest, which did not seem to him a matter of the least importance. But he noticed at the same time that the creature looked soft and good to eat. The next instant, like a ray of light flashed suddenly, he darted at it.

"But swift as he was, the pale creature's inky eyes had noted him in time. His feelers bunched suddenly tight and straight, and he shot backwards, at the same moment spouting a jet of black fluid from beneath his beaked mouth. The black jet spread instantly in a thick cloud, staining the clear, green water so deeply that Little Sword could not see through it at all. Instead of the soft flesh he had expected it to pierce, his sword met nothing but a mass of sticky anemones, shearing them from their base.

"In a fury, Little Sword dashed this way and that, trusting to luck that he would strike his elusive enemy in the darkness. But that enemy's eyes, with their enormous bulging surface and the jetty background to their lenses, could see clearly where the jewel-like eyes of the young swordfish could make out nothing. Little Sword, emerging into the half light at the edge of the cloud, was just about to give up the idle search, when something small but firm fastened itself upon his side, so sharply that it seemed to bite into the flesh.

"Little Sword's tense muscles quivered at the shock, and he gave a mighty leap which should, by all his customary reckoning, have carried him fifty feet from the spot. To his horrified amazement he did not go as many inches, nor the half of it! And then another something, small but terrible, fastened itself upon his shoulder.

"Then the black, murky cloud thinned quite away; and Little Sword saw what had happened. The pale creature, having reached a rock to which he could anchor himself with a couple of his feelers, had turned savagely upon his rash assailant. Little Sword was the prisoner of those two longer tentacles. They were trying to drag him down within reach of the other feelers, which writhed up at him like a lot of hideous snakes."

"Ugh!" cried the Babe with a shudder. "But how did they hold on to him?"

"You see," said Uncle Andy, "every feeler, long or short, had a row of saucer-shaped suckers along its underside, like the heads of those rubber-tipped arrows which I've seen you shooting at the wall, and which stick where they strike. Only *these* suckers could *hold on,* I can tell you, so fast that *you* could never have pulled off even the littlest of them.

"Little Sword looked down into the awful eyes of the Inkmaker, and realized that he had made a great mistake. But he was game all through. It was not for a swordfish, however young, to give in to any odds. Besides, just below those two great eyes, which stared up at him without ever a wink, he saw a terrible beak of a mouth, which opened and shut as if impatient to get hold of him. This sight was calculated to encourage him to exert himself, if he had needed any more encouragement than the grip of those two, pale, writhing feelers on his flesh.

"Now, for his size, Little Sword was putting up a tremendous fight. His broad, fluked tail and immense fins churned the water amazingly, and enabled him to spring this way and that in spite of all the efforts of the two long tentacles to hold him still. Nevertheless, he was slowly drawn downwards, till one of the shorter feelers reached for a hold upon him.

He darted at it, and by a lucky plunge of his sword cut its snaky tip clean off. It twisted back out of the way, like a startled worm; and Little Sword lunged at the next one. He pierced it all right, but at a point where it was so thick that the stroke did not sever it, and the tip, curling over, fastened upon him. At the same moment another feeler fixed itself upon the base of his tail, half paralyzing his struggles.

"Little Sword was now being drawn implacably downwards. In his fierce rage he struck at everything in reach, but he was too closely held to inflict any serious wounds. He was within eight or nine inches of those awful, unwinking, ink-black eyes. The great beak opened upwards at him eagerly. It looked as if his career was at an end—when the Fates of the Deep Sea decided otherwise. Apparently they had more use for Little Sword than they had for the Inkmaker. A long shadow dropped straight downward. It missed Little Sword by an inch or two. And the gaping, long-toothed jaws of an immense barracouta closed upon the head of the Inkmaker, biting him clean in halves. The blind body curled backwards spasmodically; and the tentacles, shorn off at the roots, fell aimlessly and helplessly apart. Little Sword flashed away, trailing his limp captors behind him till they dropped off. And the barracouta ate the remains of the Inkmaker at his leisure. He had no concern to those swordfish when there was tender and delicious squid to be had; for the Inkmaker, you know, was just a kind of big squid, or cuttlefish."

"But what's a barracouta?" demanded the Babe hurriedly.

"Well, he's just a fish!" said Uncle Andy. "But he's a very savage and hungry fish, some three or four feet long, with tremendous jaws like a pickerel's. And he lives only in the salt water, fortunately. *He's* not a nice fellow, either, to have around when you're swimming, I can tell you!"

"Why?" queried the Babe.

But Uncle Andy ignored the question firmly, and went on with his story.

"After this adventure Little Sword kept a very sharp look-out for the pallid, squirming tentacles, sometimes reaching out from a dark hole in the rocks or from under a mantle of seaweed, which he knew to belong to one of the Inkmakers. He hated the whole tribe with bitter hatred; but at the same time his caution was unsleeping. He bided his time for vengeance, and used his sword on crabs and flatfish and fat groupers. And so he grew at a great rate, till in the swelling sense of his power and swiftness his caution began to fade away. Even the incident itself faded from his memory, but not the hatred which had sprung from it, or the knowledge which it had taught him.

"When Little Sword was about five feet in length he carried a weapon on his snout not far from a foot long. By this time he was a great rover, hunting in the deep seas or the inshore tides as the whim of the chase might lead him, and always spoiling for a fight. He would jab his sword into the belly of a twenty-foot grampus just to relieve his feelings, and be off again before the outraged monster, bleeding through his six inches of blubber, had time to even make a pretense of charging him. And he was already a terror to the seals, who, for all their speed and dexterity, could neither catch him nor escape him.

"But he was getting a little careless. And one day, as he was sleeping, or basking, some ten feet below the surface, the broad, dark form of a sawfish arose beneath him and thrust at him with his dreadful saw. The pleasant idea of the sawfish was to rip up the sleeper's silver belly. But Little Sword awoke in time to just escape the horrid attack. He swept off in a short circle, came back with a lightning rush, and drove his sword full length into the stealthy enemy's shoulder just behind the gills. The great sawfish, heavy muscled and slow of movement, made no attempt to defend himself, but plunged suddenly downward into the gloomy depths where he loved to lie in wait. After relieving his indignation by a couple more vicious thrusts, Little Sword realized that he was too small to accomplish anything against this sneaking and prowling bulk, and shot off to look for a less dangerous basking place.

"It was soon after this close shave with the sawfish that Little Sword came once more across the path of the Inkmaker. He——"

But the Babe could contain himself no longer. He had been bursting with questions for the last ten minutes, and had heroically restrained himself. But this was too much for him.

"Why, Uncle Andy," he cried. "I thought the Inkmaker was dead. I thought the barracouta had eaten him up, feelers and eyes and all."

"Oh, you're a lot too particular!" grumbled Uncle Andy. "This was *another* Inkmaker, of course. And a very much bigger and more dangerous one, moreover, as you'll see presently. It was little *he* had to fear from the barracoutas. In fact, he had just fixed one of his longer tentacles on a vigorous four-foot barracouta, and was slowly drawing him down within reach of the rest of the feelers, when Little Sword's shining eyes alighted upon the struggle.

"This particular Inkmaker was crouching in a sort of shallow basin between rocks which were densely fringed with bright-striped weeds, starry madrepores, and sea-anemones of every lovely color. Disturbed by the struggle, however, the madrepores and anemones were nervously closing up their living blooms. The Inkmaker, who always managed somehow to have his own colors match his surroundings, so that his hideous form would not show too plainly and frighten his victims away, was now of a dirty pinkish-yellow, blotched and striped with purplish-brown; and his tentacles were like a bunch of striped snakes. Only his eyes never changed. They lay unwinking, two huge round lenses of terrible and intense blackness, staring upwards from the base of the writhing tentacles."

The Babe shuddered again, and wished that the beautiful swordfish would swim away as quickly as possible from the slimy horror. But he refrained interrupting. It would be dreadful if Uncle Andy should get annoyed and stop at this critical point!

"When Little Sword saw those long feelers dragging the barracouta down," went on Uncle Andy, after relighting his pipe, "he darted forward like a blue flame and jabbed his sword right through the nearest one."

"Oh, ho!" cried the Babe, forgetting caution. "He remembered how the barracouta had saved *him!*"

"Not much!" grunted Uncle Andy. "There's no sentiment about a swordfish, I can tell you. He'd have jabbed the barracouta, and eaten him, too, just as quick as look, but he *hated* the Inkmaker, and could not think of anything else. With a screwing backward pull he wrenched his sword out of the feeler, which seemed hardly to notice the wound. In the same instant another feeler snatched at him, for Mr. Inkmaker, you know, had ten tentacles, every one of them spoiling for a fight. It got only a slight hold, however, and Little Sword, whose strength was now something amazing, tore himself clear with a great livid, bleeding, burning patch on his side.

"And now, raging mad though he was, a gleam of sense flashed into his brain. He saw that it was not much use stabbing those tough tentacles. Lurching forward as if to stand on his head he shot straight downward, and drove his sword full length into one of those dreadful eyes.

"In an instant three or four feelers closed upon him. But they were now thrashing a little aimlessly, so that they did not work well together. The monster was confused by that terrible, searching trust. Little Sword was hampered by the feelers clutching at him, but he still had room to use his weapon. With all his weight and quivering strength he drove his sword again deep into the Inkmaker's head, twisting and wrenching it sideways as he drew it out. Other tentacles closed over him, but seemed to have lost their clutching power through the attack upon the source of their nervous energy. The struggling barracouta was drawn down with them, but blindly; and the water was now utterly black with the rank ink which the monster was pumping forth.

"For a few moments all was one boiling convulsion of fish and tentacles and ink, Little Sword simply stabbing and stabbing at the soft mass under his weapon. Then, all at once, the tentacles relaxed, falling away as slack as seaweed. The barracouta, nearly spent, swam off without even waiting to say 'Thank you.' And Little Sword coming to his senses as he realized his victory, rose slowly out of the area of the ink cloud. He knew that the Inkmaker's flesh was very good to eat, and he merely waited for the cloud to settle before making a meal which would completely satisfy his vengeance."

The Babe was thoughtful for a few moments after Uncle Andy stopped speaking. At length he said positively:

"I'm glad we don't have any Inkmakers, either, in the lake."

"Umph!" grunted Uncle Andy, "there are lots of things we don't have that we can very well do without."

CHAPTER V

ROCKED IN THE CRADLE OF THE DEEP

CASTING his flies across the eddying mouth of one of those cold streams which feed the crystal bosom of Silverwater, Uncle Andy had landed a magnificent pink-bellied trout—five pounds, if an ounce!

"Hi, but isn't he a whopper?" he cried exultantly, holding up his prize for the inspection of the Babe, who had been watching the struggle breathlessly.

"A—whopper?" repeated the Babe doubtfully. His idea of a whopper was something that objectionable little boys have been known to tell in order to get themselves out of a scrape. No full-fledged fisherman as yet, he did not see what it could have to do with a trout.

Uncle Andy seemed to divine his difficulty.

"I mean," he explained, "isn't he a big one? *Tremendous?*"

At this again the Babe looked doubtful. The fish was certainly a very beautiful one; but to the Babe's eyes it did not seem in any way remarkable for size. Yet he did not like to appear to disagree with Uncle Andy.

"Is it *big?*" he inquired politely. "Bill says there's some fish bigger than a house."

Uncle Andy looked at him askance.

"Seems to me," said he, "you're mighty hard to please to-day. And, anyhow, Bill talks nonsense. They're not fish, those monsters he was telling you about. They're *whales.*"

"But they live in the water, don't they?" protested the Babe in surprise.

"Of course!" agreed Uncle Andy, wrapping his big trout up in wet grass and seating himself on a handy log for a smoke.

"Then why aren't they fish?" persisted the Babe, ever anxious to get to the root of a matter.

"Because they're not," replied Uncle Andy, impatient at having let himself in for explanations, which he always disliked. "They're animals, just as much as a dog or a muskrat."

The Babe wrinkled his forehead in perplexity. And Uncle Andy relented.

"You see," he continued, "they're not fish, because they cannot breathe under water like fish can, but have to come to the surface for air, just as we would have to. And they're not fish, because they nurse their babies as a cow or a cat does. And—and there are lots of other reasons."

"What are the other reasons?" demanded the Babe eagerly.

But Uncle Andy had felt himself getting into deep water. He adroitly evaded the question.

"Do you suppose this old trout here," said he, pointing to the grassy bundle, "used to love and take care of its little ones, like the whale I'm going to tell you about loved and took care of hers? No indeed! The trout had hundreds of thousands, and liked nothing better than to *eat* them whenever it got the chance. But the whale had only one—at a time, that is—and she always used to think there was nothing else like it in the world. There are lots of other mothers as foolish as that. Yours, for instance, now."

The Babe laughed. It pleased him when he understood one of Uncle Andy's jokes—which was not always, by any means. He squatted himself on the moss before the log, where he could stare straight up into Uncle Andy's face with his blue, steady, expectant eyes.

"It was a long way off from Silverwater," began Uncle Andy in a far-away voice, and with a far-away look in his eyes, "that the whale calf was born. It was up North, where the summer sun swung low over a world of cold green seas, low grey shores, crumbling white ice-fields, and floating mountains of ice that flashed with lovely, fairy-like tints of palest blue and amethyst. The calf himself, with his slippery greyish-black back and under-parts of a dirty cream color, was not beautiful—though, of course, his mother thought him so, as he lay nursing just under her great fin, rocked gently by the long, slow Arctic swells."

"What's Arctic swells?" interrupted the Babe, wrinkling his forehead more than ever. He had a vision of tall, smart-looking Eskimos, in wonderful furs; and it seemed to him very curious that the old mother whale should be so tame as to let them come close enough to rock her baby for her.

"Rollers, I mean; Big waves!" grunted Uncle Andy discontentedly. "A fellow has to be so extraordinarily literal with you to-day! Now, if you interrupt again, I'll stop, and you can get Bill to tell you all about it. As I was going to say, he—the calf, not Bill—was about eight or nine feet long. He looked all head. And his head looked all mouth. And his mouth—but you could not see into that for it was very busy nursing. His mother, however, lay with her mouth half open, a vast cavern of a mouth, nearly a third the length of her body—and *it* looked all whalebone. For, you must know, she was of the ancient and honorable family of the Right Whales, who scorn to grow any teeth, and therefore must live on soup so to speak."

Here he paused, and looked at the Babe as much as to say, "Now, I suppose you're going to interrupt again, in spite of all I've said." But the Babe, restraining his curiosity about the soup, only sat staring at him with solemn eyes. So he went on.

"You see, it was a most convenient kind of

soup, a *live* soup, that they fed upon. The sea, in great spots and patches, is full of tiny creatures, sometimes jelly-fish, sometimes little squid of various kinds, all traveling in countless hosts from somewhere-or-other to somewhere else, they know not why. As the great mother whale lay there with her mouth open, these swarming little swimmers would calmly swim into it, never dreaming that it was a mouth. There they would get tangled among those long narrow strips or plates of whalebone, with their fringed edges. Every little while the whale would lazily close her mouth, thrust forward her enormous fat tongue, and force the water out through this whalebone sieve of hers. It was like draining a dish of string beans through a colander. Having swallowed the mess of jellyfish and squid, she would open her mouth again, and wait for another lot to come in. It was a very easy and comfortable way to get a bite of breakfast, while waiting for her baby to finish nursing. And every little while, from the big blowhole or nostril on top of her head she would 'spout,' or send up a spray-like jet of steamy breath. And every little while, too, the big-headed baby under her flipper would send up a baby spout, as if in imitation of his mother.

"You must not think, however, that this lazy way of feeding was enough to keep the vast frame of the mother whale (she was quite sixty feet long: three times as long as Bill's shanty yonder) supplied with food. This was just nibbling. When she felt that her baby had nursed enough, she gave it a signal which it understood. It fell a little back along her huge side. Then, lifting her enormous tail straight in the air, she dived slowly downward into the pale, greenish glimmer of the deeper tide, the calf keeping his place cleverly behind her protecting flipper.

"Down here the minute life of the ocean waters swarmed more densely than at the surface. Swimming slowly, the mother whale filled her mouth again and again with the tiny darting squid, till she had strained out and swallowed perhaps a ton of the pulpy provender. As they felt the whalebone strainers closing about them, each one took alarm and let fly a jet of inky fluid, as if thinking to hide itself from Fate; and the dim green of the surrounding water grew clouded till the calf could hardly see, and had to crowd close to his mother's side. A twist or two of her mighty flukes, like the screw of an ocean liner, drove her clear of this obscurity, and carried her, a moment later, into a packed shoal of southward journeying capelin."

The Babe's mouth opened for the natural question: "What's capelin?"

But Uncle Andy got ahead of him.

"That's a little fish something like a sardine," he explained hastily. "And they travel in such countless numbers that sometimes a storm will throw them ashore in long windrows like you see in a hay field, so that the farmers come and cart them away for manure. Well, it did not take long for the old whale to fill up even *her* great stomach, when the capelin were so numerous. She went ploughing through the shoal lazily, and stopped at last to rub her little one softly with her flipper.

"All at once she caught sight of a curious-looking creature swimming just beneath the shoal of capelin, and every now and then opening its mouth to gulp down a bushel or so of them. It was about fifteen feet long, of a ghastly grayish white color, and from its snout stood straight out a sharp, twisted horn perhaps six feet in length. It was only a stupid narwhal, with no desire in the world to offend his gigantic neighbor; but she was nervous at the sight of his horn, which made her think of her dreaded enemy the swordfish. Tucking her baby well under her fin, she made an hysterical rush at the unoffending stranger. His little pig-like eyes blinked anxiously, and, darting off at his best pace, he was speedily lost to view in the cloudy myriads of the capelin.

"Having now been under water for some twelve or fifteen minutes, the mother whale knew that it was time for her baby to breathe again—though she herself could have held on without fresh air for another five or even ten minutes without much trouble."

The Babe gasped. It was like a bad dream to him, the idea of going along without a breath.

"Oh, how it must hurt!" he burst forth. "I should think it would kill them."

"It would kill *you*, of course, in about two minutes," replied Uncle Andy. "But they are built differently. They have a handy way of doing up a lot of breathing all at once, and then not having to think any more about it for a while. You can readily see what a convenience that might be to them.

"When they got back to the surface, they lay comfortably rocking among the green swells, while they both blew all the used-up air and steam out of their lungs. The feathery little jet of the calf rose gravely beside his mother's high and graceful spout. The calf, always hungry, because he had such a lot of growing to do and was in such a hurry to do it, fell at once to nursing again, while the mother lay basking half asleep. Overhead, some great white gulls flapped and screamed against the sharp blue, now and then dropping with a splash to snatch some fish from the transparent slope of a wave. A couple of hundred yards away three seals lay basking on an ice-floe, and in the distance could be seen other whales spouting. So the mother knew that she and her baby were not alone in these wide bright spaces of sea and sky.

"As a general rule, the great whale was apt to stay not more than two or three minutes at the surface, but to spend most of her time in the moderate depths. Now, however, with her big baby to nurse, she would often linger basking at the surface till her appetite drove her to activity. In general, also, she was apt to be rather careless about keeping watch against her enemies. But now she was vigilant even when she seemed asleep, and anything the least bit out of the ordinary was enough to make her take alarm. As she lay sluggishly rocking, the great blackish round of her head and back now all awash, now rising like a reef above the waves, she suddenly caught sight of a white furry head with a black tip to its nose, swiftly cleaving the water. She knew it was only a white bear swimming, and she knew also that it was not big enough to dare attack her calf. But with her foolish mother fears she objected to its even being in the neighborhood. She swept her dark bulk around so as to hide the little one from the white swimmer's eyes, and lay glaring at him with suspicious fury. The bear, however, hardly condescended to glance at her. He was after those basking seals on the ice-floes. Presently he dived, a long, long dive, and came up suddenly at the very edge of the ice, caught the nearest seal by the throat just as they were all hurling themselves into the water.

"To this unhappy affair the old whale did not give so much as a second look. So long as the bear kept a respectful distance from her precious baby she didn't care how many silly seals he killed.

"But presently she observed, far away among her spouting kindred, the black, slow-moving shape of a steam whaler. In some past experience she had learned that these strange creatures, which seemed to have other creatures, very small, but very, very dangerous, inside of them, were the most to be dreaded of all the whale's enemies. It was at present too far off for her to take alarm, but she lay watching the incomprehensible monster so sharply that she almost forgot to blow. Presently she saw it crawl up quite close to the unsuspecting shape of one of her kinsmen. A spiteful flame leapt from its head. Then a sharp thunder came rapping across the waves, and she saw her giant kinsman hurl himself clear into the air. He fell back with a terrific splash, which set the monster rolling, and, for perhaps a minute, his struggles lashed the sea into foam. Then he lay still, and soon she saw him drawn slowly up till he clung close to the monster's side. This unheard-of action filled her with a terror that was quite sickening. Clutching her calf tremblingly under her fin she plunged once more into the deep, and, traveling as fast as posible for the little one, at a depth of perhaps two hundred feet, she headed for another feeding ground where she trusted that the monster might not follow.

"When she came again to the surface, fifteen minutes later, the monster and all her spouting kinsfolk were out of sight, hidden behind a mile-long mountain of blue ice-berg. But she was not satisfied. Remaining up less than two minutes, to give the calf time for breath, she hurriedly plunged again and continued her journey. When this manœuver had been repeated half a dozen times she began to feel more at ease. At last she came to a halt, and lay rocking in the seas just off the mouth of a spacious rock-rimmed bay.

"Here, as luck would have it, she found herself in the midst of the food which she loved best. The leaden green of the swells was all flushed and stained with pale pink. This unusual color was caused by hordes of tiny, shrimplike creatures—distant cousins of those which you like so well in a salad. The whale preferred them in the form of soup, so she went sailing slowly through them with her cavernous mouth very wide open. Every now and then she would shut her jaws and give two or three great gulps, and her little eyes, away back at the base of her skull, would almost twinkle with satisfaction.

"But, as it appeared, she was not the only one that liked shrimps. The air was full of wings and screams, where gulls, gannets, and skuas swooped and splashed, quarrelling because they got in one another's way at the feast. Also, here and there a heavy, sucking swirl on the smooth slope of a wave would show where some very big fish was taking toll of the pinky swarms. The whale kept her eye on these ponderous swirls with a certain amount of suspicion, though not really anticipating any danger here.

"She was just about coming to the conclusion that one can have enough, even of shrimps, when, glancing downwards, she caught sight of a long, slender, deadly-looking shape slanting up toward her through a space of clear water between the armies of the shrimps. She knew that grim shape all too well, and it was darting straight at her baby, its terrible sword standing out keen and straight from its pointed snout.

"In spite of her immense bulk and apparently clumsy form, the whale was capable of marvelously quick action. You see, except for her head she was all one bundle of muscle. Swift as thought, she whipped herself clear round, between her calf and the upward rush of the swordfish. She was just in time. The thrust that would have gone clean through the calf, splitting its heart in two, went deep into her own side.

"Withdrawing his terrible weapon, the robber fish whirled about like lightning and made a second dash at the coveted prize. But the mother, holding the little one tight under her flipper, wheeled again in time to intercept the attack, and again received the dreadful thrust in her own flank. So swift was the swordfish (he was a kind of giant mackerel, with all the mackerel's grace and fire and nimbleness) that he seemed to be everywhere at once. The whale was kept spinning around in a dizzy circle of foam, like a whirpool, with the bewildered calf on the inside. The mighty twisting thrusts of her tail, with its flukes twenty feet wide, set the whole surface boiling for hundreds of yards about.

"At last, grown suddenly frantic with rage, with terror for her little one, and with the pain of her wounds, the tormented mother broke into a deep booming bellow, as of a hundred bulls. The mysterious sound sent all the gulls screaming into the air, and frightened the basking walruses on the ledges three miles away. Every seal that heard it shuddered and dived, and an old white bear, prowling along the desolate beach in search of dead fish, lifted his lean head and listened nervously.

"Only the swordfish paid no attention to that tremendous and desperate cry. In the midst of it he made another rush, missed the calf by a handbreadth, and buried his sword to the socket in the mother's side.

"At this the old whale seemed to lose her wits. Still clutching the terrified calf under one flipper, she stood straight on her head, so that the head and half her body were below the surface, and fell to lashing the water all around her with ponderous, deafening blows of her tail. The huge concussions drove the swordfish from the surface, and for a minute or two he swam around her in a wide circle, about twenty feet down, trying to get the hang of these queer tactics. Then, swift and smooth as a shadow, he shot in diagonally, well below the range of those crashing strokes. His sword went clean through the body of the calf, through its heart, killing it instantly, and at the same time forcing it from its mother's hold. The lifeless but still quivering form fixed thus firmly on his sword, he darted away with it, and was instantly lost to view beyond the dense, churned hosts of the pink shrimps.

"For perhaps a minute the mother, as if bewildered by the violence of her own exertions, seemed quite unaware of what had happened. At length she stopped lashing the water, came slowly to the surface stared about her in a dazed way, and once more bellowed forth her terrible booming cry. Once more the seabirds sprang terrified to the upper air, and the old white bear on the far-off shore lifted his head once more to listen nervously."

"And she never saw her baby any more," murmured the Babe mournfully.

Uncle Andy snorted, disdaining to answer such a remark.

"Oh, I wish somebody would do something to that swordfish," continued the Babe. And he wiped a tear from his nose.

CHAPTER VI

TEDDY BEAR'S BEE TREE

THEY were exploring the high slopes of the farther shore of Silverwater. It had been an unusually long trip for the Babe's short legs, and Uncle Andy had considerately called a halt, on the pretext that it was time for a smoke. He knew that the Babe would trudge on till he dropped in his tracks before acknowledging that he was tired. A mossy boulder under the ethereal green shade of a silver birch offered the kind of resting place—comfortable yet unkempt—which appealed to Uncle Andy's taste; and there below, over a succession of three low, wooded ridges, lay outspread the enchanting mirror of the lake. Uncle Andy's pipe never tasted so good to him as when he could smoke it to the accompaniment of a wide and eye-filling view.

The Babe, who had squatted himself cross-legged on the turf at the foot of the boulder, would have appreciated that superb view also, but that his eager eyes had detected a pair of brown rabbits peering out at him inquiringly from the fringes of a thicket of young firs.

"Perhaps," he thought to himself, "if we keep very still indeed, they'll come out and play."

He was about to whisper this suggestion cautiously to Uncle Andy, when, from somewhere in the trees behind them, came a loud sound of scrambling, of claws scratching on bark, followed by a thud, a grunt, and a whining, and then the crash of some heavy creature careering through the underbrush. It paused within twenty or thirty paces of them in its noisy flight, but the bushes were so thick that they could not catch a glimpse of it.

The rabbits vanished. The Babe, startled, shrank closer to his uncle's knee, and stared up at him with round eyes of inquiry.

"He's in a hurry, all right, and doesn't care who knows it!" chuckled Uncle Andy. But his shaggy brows were knit in some perplexity.

"Who's *he?*" demanded the Babe.

"Well, now," protested Uncle Andy, as much as to say that the Babe ought to have known that without asking, "you know there's nothing in these woods big enough to make such a noise as that except a bear or a moose. And a moose can't go up a tree. You heard that fellow fall down out of a tree, didn't you?"

"Why did he fall down out of the tree?" asked the Babe, in a tone of great surprise.

"That's just what I——" began Uncle Andy. But he was interrupted.

"Oh! *Oh!* It's stung me!" cried the Babe shrilly, jumping to his feet and slapping at his ear. His eyes filled with injured tears.

Uncle Andy stared at him for a moment in grave reproof. Then he, too, sprang up as if the boulder had suddenly grown red-hot, and pawed at his hair with both hands, dropping his pipe.

"Gee! I see why he fell down!" he cried. The Babe gave another cry, clapped his hand to his leg where the stocking did not quite join the short breeches, and began hopping up and down on one foot. A heavy, pervasive hum was beginning to make itself heard.

"Come!" yelled Uncle Andy, striking at his cheek angrily and ducking his head as if he were going to butt something. He grabbed the Babe by one arm and rushed him to the fir thicket where the rabbits had been.

"Duck!" he ordered. "Down with you—flat!" And together they crawled into the low-growing, dense-foliaged thicket, where they lay side by side, face downwards.

"They won't follow us in here," murmured Uncle Andy. "They don't like thick bushes."

"But I'm afraid—we've brought some in with us, Uncle Andy," replied the Babe, trying very hard to keep the tears out of his voice. "I think I hear one squealing and buzzing in my hair. *Oh!*" And he clutched wildly at his leg.

"You're right!" said Uncle Andy, his voice suddenly growing very stern as a bee crawled over his collar and jabbed him with great earnestness in the neck. He sat up. Several other bees were creeping over him, seeking an effective spot to administer their fiery admonitions. But he paid them no heed. They stung him where they would—while he was quickly looking over the Babe's hair, jacket, sleeves, stockings, and loose little trousers. He killed half a dozen of the angry crawlers before they found a chance to do the Babe more damage.

Then he pulled out three stings, and applied moist earth from under the moss to each red and anguished spot.

The Babe looked up at him with a resolute little laugh, and shook obstinately from the tip of his nose the tears which he would not acknowledge by the attentions of his handkerchief or his fist.

"Thank you *awfully,*" he began politely. "But *oh!* Uncle Andy, your poor eye is just dreadful. Oh-h-h!"

"Yes, they *have* been getting after me a bit," agreed Uncle Andy, dealing firmly with his own assailants, now that the Babe was all right. "But this jab under the eye is the only one that matters. Here, see if you can get hold of the sting."

The Babe's keen eyes and nimble little fingers captured it at once. Then Uncle Andy plastered the spot with a daub of wet, black earth, and peered over it solemnly at the Babe's swollen ear. He straightened his grizzled hair, and tried to look as if nothing out of the way had happened.

"I wish I'd brought my pipe along," he muttered. "It's over there by the rock. But

I reckon it wouldn't be healthy for me to go and get it just yet!"

"What's made them so awful mad, do you suppose?" inquired the Babe, nursing his wounds and listening uneasily to the vicious hum which filled the air outside the thicket.

"It's that fool bear!" replied Uncle Andy. "He's struck a bee tree too tough for him to tear open, and he fooled at it just long enough to get the bees good and savage. Then he quit in a hurry. And we'll just have to stay here till the bees get cooled down."

"How long'll that be?" inquired the Babe dismally. It was hard to sit still in the hot fir thicket, with that burning, throbbing smart in his ear and two little points of fierce ache in his leg. Uncle Andy was far from happy himself; but he felt that the Babe, who had behaved very well, must have his mind diverted. He fished out a letter from his pocket, rolled himself, with his heavy pipe tobacco, a cigarette as thick as his finger, and fell to puffing such huge clouds as would discourage other bees from prying into the thicket. Then he remarked irrelevantly but consolingly:

"It isn't always, by any means, that the bees

get the best of it this way. Mostly it's the other way about. *This* bear was a fool. But there was Teddy Bear, now, a cub over the foothills of Sugar Loaf Mountain, and *he* was *not* a fool. When he tackled his first bee tree —and he was nothing but a cub, mind you—he pulled off the affair in good shape. I wish it had been *these* bees that he cleaned out."

The Babe was so surprised that he let go of his leg for a moment.

"Why?" he exclaimed, "how could a cub do what a big, strong, grown-up bear couldn't manage?" He thought with a shudder how unequal *he* would be to such an undertaking.

"You just wait and see!" admonished Uncle Andy, blowing furious clouds from his monstrous cigarette. "It was about the end of the blue-berry season when Teddy Bear lost his big, rusty-coated mother and small, glossy black sister, and found himself completely alone in the world. They had all three come down together from the high blue-berry patches to the dark swamps to hunt for roots and fungi as a variation to their fruit diet. The mother and sister had got caught together in a dead-fall—a dreadful trap which crushed them both flat in an instant. Teddy Bear, some ten feet out of danger, had stared for two seconds in frozen horror, and then raced away like mad with his mother's warning screech hoarse in his ears. He knew by instinct that he would never see the victims any more; and he was very unhappy and lonely. For a whole day he moped, roaming restlessly about the high slopes and refusing to eat, till at last he got so hungry that he just *had* to eat. Then he began to forget his grief a little, and devoted himself to the business of finding a living. But from being the most sunny-tempered of cubs he became all at once as peppery as could be.

"As I have told you," continued Uncle Andy, peering at him with strange solemnity over the mud patch beneath his swollen eye, "the blue-berries were just about done. And as Teddy would not go down to the lower lands again to hunt for other kinds of rations, he had to do a lot of hustling to find enough blue-berries for his healthy young appetite. Thus it came about that when one day, on an out-of-the-way corner of the mountain, he stumbled upon a patch of belated berries—large, plump, lapis-blue, and juicy—he fairly forgot himself in his greedy excitement. He whimpered, he grunted, he wallowed as he fed. He had no time to look where he was going. So, all of a sudden, he fell straight through a thick fringe of blue-berry bushes and went sprawling and clawing down the face of an almost perpendicular steep.

"The distance of his fall was not far short of thirty feet, and he brought up with a bump which left him not breath enough to squeal. The ground was soft, however, with undergrowth and debris, and he had no bones broken. In a couple of minutes he was busy licking himself all over to make sure he was undamaged. Reassured on this point, he went prowling in exploration of the place he had dropped into.

"It was a sort of deep bowl, not more than forty feet across at the bottom, and with its rocky sides so steep that Teddy Bear did not feel at all encouraged to climb them. He went sniffing and peering around the edges in the hope of finding some easier way of escape. Disappointed in this, he lifted his black, alert little nose, and stared longingly upwards, as if contemplating an effort to fly.

"He saw no help in that direction; but his nostrils caught a savor which for the moment put all thought of escape out of his head. It was the warm, delectable smell of honey. Teddy Bear had never tasted honey; but he needed no one to tell him it was good. Instantly he knew that he was very hungry. And instead of wanting to find a way out of the hole, all he wanted was to find out where that wonderful smell came from. If he thought any more at all of the hole, it was only to be glad he had had the great luck to fall into it.

"From the deep soil at the bottom of the hole grew three big trees, together with a certain amount of underbrush. Two of those were fir trees, green and flourishing. The third was an old maple, with several of its branches broken away. It was quite dead all down one side, while on the other only a couple of branches put forth leaves. About a small hole near the top of this dilapidated old tree Teddy Bear caught sight of a lot of bees, coming and going. Then he knew where that adorable smell came from. For though, as I think I have said, his experience was extremely limited, his mother had managed to convey to him an astonishing lot of useful and varied information.

"Teddy Bear had an idea that bees, in spite of their altogether diminutive size, were capable of making themselves unpleasant, and also that they had a temper which was liable to go off at half-cock. Nevertheless, being a bear of great decision, he lost no time in wondering what he had better do. The moment he had convinced himself that the honey was up that tree, up that tree he went to get it."

"Oh!" cried the Babe, in tones of shuddering sympathy, as he felt at his leg and his ear. "Oh! why *didn't* he stop to think?"

Uncle Andy did not seem to consider that this remark called for any reply. He ignored it. Stopping just at this critical point he proceeded with exasperating deliberation to roll himself another fat and clumsy cigarette. Then he applied fresh earth to both the Babe's stings and his own. At last he went on.

"That tree must have been hollow a long way down, for almost as soon as Teddy Bear's claws began to rattle on the bark the bees suspected trouble and began to get excited. When he was not much more than halfway up, and hanging to the rough bark with all his claws, *biff!*—something sharp and very hot struck him in the nose. He grunted, and almost let go in his surprise. Naturally, he wanted to paw his nose—for *you* know how it smarted!"

"I guess *so!*" murmured the Babe in deepest sympathy, stroking the patch of mud on his ear.

"But that cub had naturally a level head. He knew that if he let go with even one paw he would fall to the ground, because the trunk of the tree at that point was so big he could not get a good hold upon it. So he just dug his smarting nose into the bark and clawed himself around to the other side of the tree, where the branches that were still green sheltered him a bit, and there was a thick shadow from the nearest fir tree, whose boughs interwove with those of the maple. Here the bees didn't seem to notice him. He kept very still, listening to their angry buzz till it had somewhat quieted down. Then, instead of going about it with a noisy dash, as he had done before, he worked his way up stealthily and slowly till he could crawl into the crotch of the first branch. You see, that bear could learn a lesson.

"Presently he stuck his nose around to see how near he was to the bees' hole. He had just time to locate it—about seven or eight feet above him—when again *biff!* And he was stung on the lip. He drew in his head again quick, I can tell you—quick enough to catch that bee and smash it. He *ate* it, indignantly. And then he lay curled up in the crotch for some minutes, gently pawing his sore little snout and whimpering angrily.

"The warm, sweet smell of the honey was very strong up there. And, moreover, Teddy Bear's temper was now thoroughly aroused. Most cubs, and some older bears, would have relinquished the adventure at this point, for, as a rule, it takes a wise old bear to handle a bee tree successfully. But Teddy Bear was no ordinary cub, let me tell you. He lay nursing his anger and his nose till he had made up his mind what to do. And then he set out to do it.

"Hauling himself up softly from branch to branch, he made no more noise than a shadow. As soon as he was right behind the bees' hole he reached around, dug his claws into the edge of it, and pulled with all his might. The edges were rotten, and a pawful of old wood came. So did the bees!

"They were onto him in a second. He grunted furiously, screwed his eyes up tight, tucked his muzzle down under his left arm—which was busy holding on—and reached around blindly for another pull. This time he got a good grip, and he could feel something give. But the fiery torture was too much for him. He drew in his paw, crouched back into the crotch, and cuffed wildly at his own ears and face as well as at the air, now thick with his assailants. The terrific hum they made somewhat daunted him. For a few seconds he stood his ground, battling frantically. Then, with an agility that you would never have dreamed his chubby form to be capable of, he went swinging down from branch to branch, whining and coughing and spluttering and squealing all the way. From the lowest branch he slid down the trunk, his claws tearing the bark and just clinging enough to break his fall.

"Reaching the ground, he began to roll himself over and over in the dry leaves and twigs till he had crushed out all the bees that clung in his fur."

"But why didn't the rest of the bees follow him? They followed this other bear to-day!" protested the Babe feelingly.

"Well, they didn't!" returned Uncle Andy quite shortly, with his customary objection to being interrupted. Then he thought better of it, and added amiably: "That's a sensible question—a very natural question; and I'll give you the answer to it in half a minute. I've got to tell you my yarn in my own way, you know—you ought to know it by this time—but you'll see presently just why the bees acted so differently in the two cases.

"Well, as soon as Teddy Bear had got rid of his assailants he clawed down through the leaves and twigs and moss—like *I* did just now, you remember, till he came to the damp, cool earth. Ah, how he dug his smarting muzzle into it, and rooted in it, and rubbed it into his ears and on his eyelids! till pretty soon—for the bee stings do not poison a bear's blood as strongly as they poison us—he began to feel much easier. As for the rest of his body—

well, *those* stings didn't amount to much, you know, because his fur and his hide were both so thick.

"At last he sat up on his haunches and looked around. You should have seen him!"

"I'm glad I wasn't there, Uncle Andy," said the Babe, earnestly shaking his head. But Uncle Andy paid no attention to the remark.

"His muddy paws drooped over his breast, and his face was all stuck over with leaves and moss and mud——"

"*We* must look funny, too," suggested the Babe, staring hard at the black mud poultice under his uncle's swollen eye. But his uncle refused to be diverted.

"And his glossy fur was in a state of which his mother would have strongly disapproved. But his twinkling little eyes burned with wrath and determination. He sniffed again that honey smell. He stared up at the bee tree, and noted that the opening was much larger than it had been before his visit. A big crack extended from it for nearly two feet down the trunk. Moreover, there did not seem to be so many bees buzzing about the hole."

The Babe's eyes grew so round with inquiry

at this point that Uncle Andy felt bound to explain.

"You see, as soon as the bees got it into their cunning heads that their enemy was going to succeed in breaking into their storehouse, they decided that it was more important to save their treasures than to fight the enemy. It's like when one's house is on fire. At first one fights to put the fire out. When that's no use, then one thinks only of saving the things. That's the principle the bees generally go upon. At first they attack the enemy, in the hope of driving him off. But if they find that he is going to succeed in breaking in and burglarizing the place, then they fling themselves on the precious honey which they have taken so much pains to store, and begin to stuff their honey sacks as full as possible. All they think of then is to carry away enough to keep them going while they are getting established in new quarters. The trouble with the fool bear who has got us into this mess to-day was that he tackled a bee tree where the outside wood was too strong for him to rip open. The bees knew he couldn't get in at them, so they all turned out after him, to give him a good lesson. When he got away through the underbrush so quickly they just turned on us, because they felt they must give a lesson to somebody."

"*We* didn't want to steal their old honey," muttered the Babe in an injured voice.

"Oh, I'm not so sure!" said Uncle Andy. "I shouldn't wonder if Bill and I'd come over here some night and smoke the rascals out. But we can wait. That's the difference between us and Teddy Bear. He wouldn't even wait to clean the leaves off his face, he was so anxious for that honey, and his revenge.

"This time he went up the tree slowly and quietly, keeping out of sight all the way. When he was exactly on a level with the entrance he braced himself solidly, reached his right paw around the trunk like lightning, got a fine hold on the edge of the new crack, and wrenched with all his might.

"A big strip of half-rotten wood came away so suddenly that Teddy Bear nearly fell out of the tree.

"A lot of bees came with it; and once more Teddy Bear's head was in a swarm of little darting, piercing flames. But his blood was up. He held onto that chunk of bee tree. A big piece of comb, dripping with honey and crawling with bees, was sticking to it. Whimpering and pawing at his face, he crunched a great mouthful of the comb, bees and all.

"Never had he tasted, never had he dreamed of, anything so delicious! What was the pain of his smarting muzzle to that ecstatic mouthful? He snatched another, which took all the rest of the comb. Then he flung the piece of wood to the ground.

"The bees, meanwhile—except those which had stung him and were now crawling, stingless and soon to die, in his fur—had suddenly left him. The whole interior of their hive was exposed to the glare of daylight, and their one thought now was to save all they could. Teddy Bear's one thought was to seize all he could. He clawed himself around boldly to the front of the tree, plunged one greedy paw straight into the heart of the hive, snatched forth a big, dripping, crawling comb, and fell to munching it up as fast as possible—honey, bees, brood-comb, bee-bread, all together indiscriminately. The distracted bees paid him no

"His little round stomach was swollen with honey, so he didn't care a cent."

more attention. They were too busy filling their honey sacks."

The Babe smacked his lips. He was beginning to get pretty hungry himself.

"Well," continued Uncle Andy, "Teddy Bear chewed and chewed, finally plunging his whole head into the sticky mess—getting a few stings, of course, but never thinking of them—till he was just so gorged that he couldn't hold another morsel. Then, very slowly and heavily, grunting all the time, he climbed down the bee tree. He felt that he wanted to go to sleep. When he reached the bottom he sat up on his haunches to look around for some sort of a snug corner. His eyelids were swollen with stings, but his little round stomach was swollen with honey, so he didn't care a cent. His face was all daubed with honey, and earth, and leaves, and dead bees. His whole body was a sight. And his claws were so stuck up with honey and rotten wood and bark that he kept opening and shutting them like a baby who has got a feather stuck to its fingers and doesn't know what to do with it. But he was too sleepy to bother about his appearance. He just waddled over to a sort of nook between the roots of the next tree, curled up with his sticky nose between his sticky paws, and was soon snoring."

"And did he ever get out of that deep hole?" inquired the Babe, always impatient of the abrupt way in which Uncle Andy was wont to end his stories.

"Of course he got out. He climbed out," answered Uncle Andy. "Do you suppose a bear like that could be kept shut up long? And now I think *we* might be getting out, too! I don't hear any more humming outside, so I reckon the coast's about clear."

He peered forth cautiously.

"It's all right. Come along," he said. "And there's my pipe at the foot of the rock, just where I dropped it," he added, in a tone of great satisfaction. Then, with mud-patched, swollen faces, and crooked but cheerful smiles, the two refugees emerged into the golden light of the afternoon, and stretched themselves. But, as Uncle Andy surveyed first the Babe and then himself in the unobstructed light, his smile faded.

"I'm afraid Bill's going to have the laugh on us when we get home!" said he.

CHAPTER VII

THE SNOWHOUSE BABY

THERE had been a film of glass-clear ice that morning all round the shores of Silverwater. It had melted as the sun climbed high into the bland October blue; but in the air remained, even at midday, a crispness, a tang, which set the Child's blood tingling. He drew the spicy breath of the spruce forests as deep as possible into his little lungs, and outraged the solemn silences with shouts and squeals of sheer ecstasy, which Uncle Andy had not the heart to suppress. Then, all at once, he remembered what the thrilling air, the gold and scarlet of the trees, the fairy ice films, the whirr of the partridge wings, and the sharp cries of the bluejays all meant. It meant that soon Uncle Andy would take him back to town, the cabin under the hemlock would be boarded up, Bill the Guide would go off to the lumber camps beyond the Ottanoonsis, and Silverwater would be left to the snow and the solitude of winter. His heart tightened with homesickness. Yet, after all, he reflected, during the months of cold his beloved Silverwater would be none too friendly a place, especially to such of the little furred and feathered folk as were bold enough to linger about its shores. He shivered as he thought of the difference winter must make to all the children of the wild.

"Why so solemn all of a sudden?" asked Uncle Andy, eyeing him suspiciously. "I thought a minute ago you'd take the whole roof off the forest an' scare the old bull moose across the lake into shedding his new antlers."

"I was just thinking," answered the Child.

"And does it hurt?" inquired Uncle Andy politely.

But, young as he was, the Child had learned to ignore sarcasm—especially Uncle Andy's, which he seldom understood.

"I was just wondering," he replied, shaking his head thoughtfully, "what the young ones of all the wild creatures would do in the winter to keep warm. Bill says they all go to sleep. But I don't see how *that* keeps them warm, Uncle Andy."

"Oh, *Bill!*" remarked Uncle Andy, in a tone which stripped all Bill's statements of the last shreds of authority. "But, as a matter of fact, there *aren't* many youngsters around in the woods in winter—not enough for you to be looking so solemn about. They're mostly born early enough in spring and summer to be pretty well grown up by the time winter comes on them."

"Gee!" murmured the Child enviously. "I wish I could get grown up as quick as that."

Uncle Andy sniffed.

"There are lots of people besides you," said he, "that don't know when they're well off. But," he continued, seating himself on Bill's chopping log and meditatively cleaning out his pipe bowl with a bit of chip, "there *are* some youngsters who have a fashion of getting themselves born right in the worst of the cold weather—and that not here in Silverwater neither, but way up north, where weather is weather, let me tell you—where it gets so cold that, if you were foolish enough to cry, the tears would all freeze instantly, till your eyes were shut up in a regular ice jam."

"I wouldn't cry," declared the Child.

"No? But I don't want you to interrupt me any more."

"Of course not," said the Child politely. Uncle Andy eyed him searchingly, and then decided to go on.

"Away up north," he began abruptly—and paused to light his pipe—"away up north, as I was saying, it was just midwinter. It was also midnight—which, in those latitudes, is another way of saying the same thing. The land as far as eye could see in every direction was flat, dead white, and smooth as a table, except for the long curving windrows into which the hard snow had been licked up by weeks of screaming wind. Just now the wind was still. The sky was like black steel sown with diamonds, and the stars seemed to snap under the terrific cold. Suddenly their bitter sparkle faded, and a delicate pale green glow spread itself, opening like a fan, till it covered half the heavens. Almost immediately the center of the base of the fan rolled itself up till the strange light became an arch of intense radiance, the green tint shifting rapidly to blue-white, violet, gold, and cherry rose. A moment more and the still arch broke up into an incalculable array of upright spears of light, pointing toward the zenith, and dancing swiftly from side to side with a thin, mysterious rustle. They danced so for some minutes, ever changing color, till suddenly they all melted back into the fan-shaped glow. And the glow remained, throbbing softly as if breathless, uncertain whether to die away or to go through the whole performance again."

"I know——" began the Child, but checked himself at once with a deprecating glance of apology.

"Except for the dancing wonder of the light," continued Uncle Andy, graciously pretending not to hear the interruption, "nothing stirred in all that emptiness of naked space. Of life there was not the least sign anywhere. This appeared the very home of death and intolerable cold. Yet at one spot, between two little, almost indistinguishable ridges of snow, might have been noticed a tiny wisp of vapor. If one had put his face down close to the snow, so that the vapor came between his eyes and the light, he would have made it out quite distinctly. And it would have certainly seemed very puzzling that anything like steam should be coming up out of that iron-bound expanse."

Now the Child had once seen, in the depth of winter, a wreath of mist arising from the snowy rim of an open spring, and for the life of him he could not hold his tongue.

"It was a boiling spring," he blurted out.

Uncle Andy gazed at him for some seconds in a disconcerting silence, till the Child felt himself no bigger than a minute.

"It was a bear," he announced at length coldly. Then he was silent again.

And the Child, mortified at having made such a bad guess, was silent too, in spite of his pangs of curiosity at this startling assertion.

"You see," went on Uncle Andy, after he was satisfied that the Child was not going to interrupt again, at least for the moment, "you see, under those two ridges of frozen snow there was a little cavern-like crevice in the rock. It was sheltered perfectly from those terrific winds which sometimes for days together would drive screaming over the levels. And in this crevice, at the first heavy snowfall, a big white bear had curled herself up to sleep.

"She had had a good hunting season, with plenty of seals and salmon to eat, and she was fat and comfortable. Though very drowsy, she did not go quite to sleep at once, but for several days, in a dreamy half-doze, she kept from time to time turning about and rearranging her bed. All the time the snow was piling down into the crevice, till at last it was level full and firmly packed. And in the meantime the old bear, in her sleepy turnings, had managed to make herself a sort of snowhouse—decidedly narrow, indeed, but wonderfully snug in its way. There was no room to take exercise, of course, but that, after all, was about the last thing she was thinking of. A day or two more and she was too fast asleep to do anything but breathe.

"The winter deepened, and storm after storm scourged the naked plain; and the snow fell endlessly, till the snowhouse was buried away fairly out of remembrance. The savage cold swept down noiselessly from outer space, till, if there had been any such things as thermometers up there, the mercury would have been frozen hard as steel and the thin spirit to a sticky, ropy syrup. But even such cold as that could not get down to the hidden snowhouse where the old bear lay so sound asleep."

The Child wagged his head wistfully at the picture, and then cheered himself with the resolve to build just such a snowhouse in the back yard that winter—if only there should fall enough snow. But he managed to hold his tongue about it.

"Just about the middle of the winter," went on Uncle Andy, after a pause to see if the Child was going to interrupt him again, "the old bear began to stir a little. She grumbled, and whimpered, and seemed to be having uneasy dreams for a day or two. At last she half woke up—or perhaps a little more than half. Then a little furry cub was born to her. She was just about wide enough awake to tell him how glad she was to see him and have him with her, and to lick him tenderly for a while, and to get him nursing comfortably. When she had quite satisfied herself that he was a cub to do her credit, she dozed off to sleep again without any anxiety whatever. You see, there was not the least chance of his being stolen, or falling downstairs, or getting into any mischief whatever. And that was where she had a great advantage over lots of mothers whom we could think of if we tried."

"But what made the steam, Uncle Andy?" broke in the Child, somewhat irrelevantly. He had a way, sometimes rather exasperating to the narrator, of never forgetting the loose ends in a narrative, and of calling attention to them at unexpected moments.

"Can't you see that for yourself?" grunted Uncle Andy impatiently. "It was *breath.* Try to think for yourself a little. Well, as I was trying to say, there was nothing much for the cub to do in the snowhouse but nurse, sleep, and grow. To these three important but not exciting affairs he devoted himself entirely. Neither to him nor to his big white mother did it matter in the least whether the long Arctic gales roared over their unseen roof, or the unimaginable Arctic cold groped for them with noiseless fingers. Neither foe could reach them in their warm refuge. Nothing at all, indeed, could find them, except, once in a while, when the Northern Lights were dancing with unusual brilliance across the sky, a dim, pallid glow, which would filter down through the snow and allow the cub's eyes (if they happened to be open at the time) to make out something of his mother's gigantic white form.

"For the youngster of so huge a mother, the snowhouse baby was quite absurdly small. But this defect, by sticking closely to his business, he remedied with amazing rapidity. In fact, if his mother had cared to stay awake long enough to watch, she could fairly have seen him grow. But, of course, this growth was all at his mother's expense, seeing that he had no food except her milk. So as he grew bigger and fatter, she grew thinner and lanker, till you would hardly have recognized this long, gaunt, white fur bag of bones for the plump beast of the previous autumn.

"But all passes—even an Arctic winter. The sun began to make short daily trips across the horizon. It got higher and higher, and hotter and hotter. The snow began to melt, crumble, shrink upon itself. Up to within a couple of hundred yards of the hidden snowhouse, what had seemed to be solid land broke up and revealed itself as open sea, crowded with huge ice cakes, and walrus, and seals. Sea birds came splashing and screaming. And a wonderful thrill awoke in the air.

"That thrill got down into the snowhouse—the roof of which was by this time getting much thinner. The cub found himself much less sleepy. He grew restless. He wanted to stretch his sturdy little legs to find out what they were good for. His mother, too, woke up. She found herself so hungry that there was no temptation to go to sleep again. Moreover, it was beginning to feel too warm for comfort—that is, for a polar bear's comfort, not for yours or mine—in the snowhouse. She got up and shook herself. One wall of the snowhouse very civilly gave way a bit, allowing her more room. But the roof, well supported by the rock, still held. The snowhouse was full of a beautiful pale-blue light.

"Just at this particular moment a little herd of walrus—two old bulls and four cows with their fat, oily-looking calves—came sprawling, floundering and grunting by. They were quite out of place on land, of course, but for some reason known only to themselves they were crossing over the narrow neck of low ground from another bay, half a mile away. Perhaps the ice pack had been jammed in by wind and current on that side, filling the shallow bay to the bottom and cutting the walrus off from their feeding grounds. If not that, then it was some other equally urgent reason, or the massive beasts, who can move on land only by a series of violent and exhausting flops, would never have undertaken an enterprise so formidable as a half-mile overland journey. They were accomplishing it, however, with a vast deal of groaning and wheezing and deep-throated grunting, when they arrived at the end of the crevice wherein the snowhouse baby and his mother were concealed.

"Lifting their huge, whiskered and tusked heads, and plunging forward laboriously on their awkward flippers, the two old bulls went by, followed by the ponderous cows with their lumpy, rolling calves. The hindermost cow, a few feet to the right of the herd, came so close to the end of the crevice that the edge of the snow gave way and her left flipper slipped into it, throwing her forward upon her side. As she struggled to recover herself, close beside her the snow was heaved up, and a terrible, grinning white head emerged, followed by gigantic shoulders and huge, claw-armed, battling paws.

"This sudden and dreadful apparition startled the walrus cow into new vigor, so that with a convulsive plunge she tore herself free of the pitfall. For a couple of seconds the old bear towered above her, with sagacious eyes taking in the whole situation. Then, judiciously ignoring the mother, she sprang over her, treading her down into the snow, fell upon the fat calf, and with one tremendous buffet broke its neck.

"With a hoarse roar of grief and fury the cow wheeled upon her haunches, reared her sprawling bulk aloft, and tried to throw herself upon the slayer. The bear nimbly avoided the shock, and whirled round to see where her cub was. Blinking at the light and dazed by the sudden uproar, but full of curiosity, he was just crawling up out of the ruins of the snowhouse. His mother dragged him forth by the scruff of the neck, and with a heave of one paw sent him rolling over and over along the snow, a dozen paces out of danger. At the same time something in her savage growls conveyed to him a first lesson in that wholesome fear which it is so well for the children of the wild to learn early. As he pulled himself together and picked himself up he was still full of curiosity, but at the same time he realized the absolute necessity for keeping out of the way of something, whatever it was.

"He soon saw what it was. At the cry of the bereaved mother the two great walrus bulls had turned. Now, with curious, choked roars, which seemed to tear their way with difficulty out of their deep chests, they came floundering back to the rescue. The cub, a sure instinct asserting itself at once, looked behind him to see that the path of escape was clear. Then he sat up on his haunches, his twinkling little eyes shifting back and forth between those mighty oncoming bulks and the long, gaunt, white form of his mother.

"For perhaps half a minute the old bear stood her ground, dodging the clumsy but terrific onslaughts of the cow, and dealing her two or three buffets which would have smashed in the skeleton of any creature less tough than a walrus or an elephant. But she had no notion of risking her health and the future of her baby by cultivating any more intimate acquaintance with those two roaring mountains of blubber which were bearing down upon her. When they were within just one more crashing plunge, she briskly drew aside, whirled about, and trotted off to join her cub. They were really so clumsy and slow, those walruses, that she hardly cared to hurry.

"For a few yards the two bulls pursued her; so she and the cub strolled off together to a distance of some fifty paces, and there halted to see what would happen next. Even creatures so dull-witted as those walrus bulls could see they would waste their time if they undertook to chase bears on dry land, so they turned back, grumbling under their long tusks, and joined the cow in inspecting the body of the dead calf. Soon coming to the conclusion that it was quite too dead to be worth bothering about, they all three went floundering on after the other cows, who had by this time got their own calves safely down to the water, and were swimming about anxiously, as if they feared that the enemy might follow them even into their own element. Then, after as brief an interval as discretion seemed to require, the old bear led the way back, sniffed at the body of the fat walrus calf, and crouched down beside it with a long *woof* of deepest satisfaction. For it is not often, let me tell you, that a polar bear, ravenous after her long winter's fast, is lucky enough to make a kill like that just at the very moment of coming out of her den."

Uncle Andy knocked the ashes out of his pipe with that air of finality which the Child knew so well, and sometimes found so disappointing.

"But what became of the snowhouse baby?" he urged.

"Oh," replied Uncle Andy, getting up from the chopping-log, "you see, he was no longer a snowhouse baby, because the snowhouse was all smashed up, and also rapidly melting. Moreover, it was no longer winter, you know; so he was just like lots of other wild babies, and went about getting into trouble, and getting out again, and growing up, till at last, when he was almost half as big as herself and *perfectly* well able to take care of himself, his mother chased him away and went off to find another snowhouse."

CHAPTER VIII

LITTLE SILK WING

THE first of the twilight over Silverwater. So ethereal were the thin washes of palest orange and apple-green reflection spreading over the surface of the lake, out beyond the fringe of alder bushes, so bubble-like in delicacy the violet tones of the air among the trees, just fading away into the moth-wing brown of dusk, that the Child was afraid to ask even the briefest questions, lest his voice should break the incomparable enchantment. Uncle Andy sat smoking, his eyes withdrawn in a dream. From the other side of the point, quite out of sight, where Bill was washing the dishes after the early camp supper, came a soft clatter of tins. But the homely sound had no power to jar the quiet.

The magic of the hour took it, and transmuted it, and made it a note in the chord of the great stillness. From the pale greenish vault of sky came a long, faint twang as of a silver string, where the swoop of a night hawk struck the tranced air to a moment's vibration. A minute or two later the light splash of a small trout leaping, and then, from the heart of the hemlock wood further down the shore, the mellow *hoo-hoo-hoo-oo* of a brown owl.

The Child was squatting on the mossy turf and staring out, round-eyed, across the water. Suddenly he jumped, clapped both grimy little hands to his face, and piped a shrill "Oh!" A bat's wing had flittered past his nose so close that he might have caught it in his teeth if he had wanted to—*and* been quick enough.

Uncle Andy turned, took his pipe from his mouth with marked deliberation, and eyed the Child severely.

"What on earth's the matter?" he inquired, after a disapproving pause.

"I thought it was trying to bite my nose," explained the Child apologetically.

"There's not very much to bite, you know," said Uncle Andy, in a carping mood at having had his reveries disturbed.

"I know it's pretty little, and turns up—

rather," agreed the Child; "but I don't want anything to bite it."

"Nonsense!" said Uncle Andy. "Who'd want to?"

"It was that bat!" declared the Child, pointing to the shadowy form zigzagging over the fringe of bushes at the edge of the water. "He came down and hit me right in the face —almost."

"That bat bite you!" retorted Uncle Andy with a sniff of scorn. "Why, he was doing you the most friendly turn he knew how. No doubt there was a big mosquito just going to bite you, and that little chap there snapped it up in time to save you. There are lots of folk beside bats that get themselves misunderstood just when they are trying hardest to do some good."

"Oh, I see!" murmured the Child politely—which, of course, meant that he did not see at all what Uncle Andy was driving at. "*Why* do bats get themselves misunderstood, Uncle Andy?"

His uncle eyed him narrowly. He was always suspecting the Child of making game of him—than which nothing could be further from the Child's honest and rather matter-of-fact intentions. The question, to be sure, was rather a poser. While he pondered a reply to it—apparently absorbed in the task of relighting his pipe—the Child's attention was diverted. And forever the question of why bats get themselves misunderstood remained unanswered.

The bat chanced at the moment to be zigzagging only a dozen feet or so away, when from the empty air above, as if created on the instant out of nothingness, dropped a noiseless, shadowy shape of wings. It seemed to catch the eccentric little flutterer fairly. But it didn't—for the bat was a marvelous adept at dodging. With a lightning swerve it emerged from under the great wings and darted behind Uncle Andy's head. The baffled owl, not daring to come so near the hated man-creatures, winnowed off in ghostly silence.

At the same moment a tiny, quivering thing, like a dark leaf, floated to the ground. There, instead of lying quiet like a leaf, it fluttered softly.

"What's *that*?" demanded the Child.

"Hush!" ordered Uncle Andy in a peremptory whisper.

The shadowy leaf on the ground continued to flutter, as if trying to rise into the air. Presently the bat reappeared and circled over it. A moment more and it dropped, touched the ground for a second with wide, uplifted wings, and then sailed off again on a long, swift, upward curve. The fluttering, shadowy leaf had disappeared.

For once the Child had no questions ready. He had so much to ask about all at once. His eyes like saucers with interrogation, he turned appealingly to his uncle and said nothing.

"That was the little one—one of the two little ones," said Uncle Andy obligingly.

"But what?—why?——"

"You see," went on Uncle Andy, hastening to explain before he could be overwhelmed, "your poor little friend was a mother bat, and she was carrying her two young ones with her, clinging to her neck with their wings, while she was busy hunting gnats and moths and protecting your nose from mosquitoes. When the owl swooped on her, and so nearly caught her, she dodged so violently that one of the little ones was jerked from its hold. Being too young to fly, it could do nothing but flutter to the ground and squat there, beating its wings till the mother came to look for it. How she managed to pick it up again so neatly, I can't say. But you saw for yourself how neat it was, eh?"

The Child nodded his head vigorously and smacked his lips in agreement.

"But why does she carry them around with her that way?" he inquired. "It seems to me awfully dangerous. I don't think *I'd* like it."

He pictured to himself his own substantial mamma swooping erratically through the air, with skirts flying out behind and himself clinging precariously to her neck. And at the thought he felt a sinking sensation at the pit of his stomach.

"Well, you know, you're not a bat," said Uncle Andy sententiously. "If you were you'd probably think it much pleasanter, and far *less* dangerous, than being left at home alone while your mother was out swooping 'round after moths and June bugs.' "

"Why?" demanded the Child promptly.

"Well, you just listen a bit," answered Uncle

Andy in his exasperating way. He hated to answer any of the Child's most innocent questions directly if he could get at them in a roundabout way. "Once upon a time"—("Ugh!" thought the Child to himself, "*this* is going to be a fairy story!" But it wasn't). "Once upon a time," went on Uncle Andy slowly, "there was a young bat—a baby bat so small you might have put him into your mother's thimble. He lived high up in the peak of the roof of an old barn down in the meadows beside the golden, rushing waters of the Nashwaak stream, not more than five or six miles from Fredericton. We'll call him Little Silk Wing."

"*I*'ve been to Fredericton!" interjected the Child with an important air.

"Really!" said Uncle Andy. "Well, Little Silk Wing hadn't. And now, who's going to tell this story, you or I?"

"I won't interrupt any more!" said the Child penitently. "But why was he called Little Silk Wing, Uncle Andy?"

His uncle looked at him in despair. Then he answered, with unwonted resignation, "His wings weren't really any silkier than those of his tiny sister. But he got hold of the name *first,* that's all. So it was his!

"When the two were first born they were so tiny as to be quite ridiculous—little shriveled, pale mites, that could do nothing but hang to their mother's breasts, and nurse diligently, and grow. They grew almost at once to the same color as their mother, plumped out till they were so big as to be not quite lost in a thimble and developed a marvelous power of clinging to their mother's body while she went careering through the air in her dizzy evolutions.

But when they were big enough for their weight to be a serious interference with their mother's hunting, then she was forced, most reluctantly, to leave them at home sometimes. She would take them both together into the narrow crevice between the top beam and the slope of the roof, and there they would lie motionless, shrouded in their exquisitely fine, mouse-colored wing membranes, and looking for all the world like two little bits of dry wood. It was not always lonely for them, because there were usually at least two or three grown-up bats hanging by their toes from the edge of a nearby crack, taking brief rest from the toil of their aerial chase. But it was always monotonous, unless they were asleep. For all movement was rigorously forbidden them, as being liable to betray them to some foe."

"Why, what could get at them, away up there?" demanded the Child, to whom the peak of a lead always seemed the remotest, most inaccessible, and most mysterious of spots.

"Wait and see!" answered Uncle Andy, with the air of an oracle. "Well, one night a streak of moonlight, like a long white finger, came in through a crack above and lit up those two tiny huddled shapes in their crevice. It came so suddenly upon them that Little Silk Wing, under the touch of that blue-white radiance, stirred uneasily and half unfolded his wings. The movement caught the great, gleaming eyes of an immense brown hunting spider who chanced at that moment to be prowling down the underside of the roof. He was one of the kind that does not spin webs, but catches its prey by stealing up and pouncing upon it. He knew that a little bat, when young enough, was no stronger than a big butterfly, and its blood would be quite good enough to suck. Stealthily he crept down into the brightness of that narrow ray, wondering whether the youngster was too big for him to tackle or not. He made up his mind to have a go at it. In fact, he was just gathering his immense, hairy legs beneath him for that fatal pounce of his, when he was himself pounced upon by a flickering shadow, plucked from his place, paralyzed by a bite through the thorax, and borne off to be devoured at leisure by a big bat which had just come in."

"Oh, I see," muttered the Child feelingly. He was himself a good deal afraid of spiders, and he meant that he understood now why it was less dangerous for little bats to go swinging wildly through the twilight clinging to their mother's necks than to stay at home alone.

But Uncle Andy paid no heed to the interruption.

"On the following night," he continued, "Little Silk Wing and his sister found themselves once more alone in the crevice at the end of the beam. They knew nothing of the peril from which they had been saved the night before, so they had learned no lesson. On this night they were restless, for their mother had fluttered away, leaving them both a little hungry. Hunting had been bad, and she had somewhat less milk for them than their growing appetites demanded. When once more that slender finger of moonlight, feeling its way through a chink in the roof, fell upon them in their crevice, it was the little sister this time that stirred and fluttered under its ghostly touch. She stretched one wing clear out upon the beam, and it was with difficulty that she restrained herself from giving vent to one of her infinitesimally thin squeaks, tiny as a bead that would drop through the eye of a needle.

"There was no great prowling spider to catch sight of her to-night. But a very hungry mouse, as it chanced, was just at that moment tip-toeing along the beam, wondering what he could find that would be good to eat. A lump of toasted cheese, or an old grease rag, or a well-starched collar, or a lump of cold suet pudding would have suited him nicely, but inexorable experience had taught him that such delicacies were seldom to be found in the roof of the barn. Under the circumstances, any old moth or beetle or spider, dead or alive, would be better than nothing.

How his little black, beadlike eyes glistened as they fell upon that frail membrane of a wing fluttering on the beam! He darted forward, straight and swift as a weaver's shuttle, seized the delicate wing in his strong white teeth, and dragged the baby bat from her hiding place. Baby as she was, she was game. For one moment she sat up and chattered angry defiance, in a voice like the winding of a watch, but so thin and high-pitched that only a fine ear could have caught it. Then the mouse seized her, bit her tiny neck through, and dragged her off, sprawling limply, along the beam."

The Child nodded vigorously. He needed nothing more to convince him of the superior security of a life of travel and adventure, as compared with the truly appalling perils of staying at home.

"I see you take me!" said Uncle Andy approvingly. "But this, as you will observe, was not Little Silk Wing, but his sister. For Little Silk Wing life became now more interesting.

Having only one baby left, his mother was able to carry him with her wherever she went. And she would not have left him alone again for the world, lest the unknown but dreadful fate which had befallen his sister should overtake him also.

He was old enough and wide awake enough by this time to appreciate his advantages. He could feel the thrill of his mother's long, swinging swoops through the dewy coolness of the dusk. He could thrill in sympathy with her excitement of the chase, when she went fluttering up into the thin pallor of the upper air, following inexorably the desperate circlings of some high-flying cockchafer. When she dropped like lead to snap up some sluggish night moth, its wings were not yet quite dry from the chrysalis, as he clung to the swaying grass tops, his tiny eyes sparkled keenly. And when she went zigzagging, with breathless speed and terrifying violence, to evade the noiseless attack of the brown owl, he hung on to her neck with the tenacity of despair and imagined that their last hour had come. But it hadn't, for his mother was clever and expert. She had fooled many owls in her day.

This adventurous life of his, of course, was lived entirely at night. During the day he slept, for the most part, folded in his mother's wing membranes, while she hung by her toes from the edge of a warped board in the warm goldy-brown shadows of the peak of the old barn. Outside, along the high ridge pole, swallows, king birds, jays, and pigeons gathered under the bright blue day to scream, chatter or coo their ideas of life, each according to the speech of its kind. And sometimes a cruel-eyed, hook-beaked, trim, well-bred looking hawk would perch there on the roof—quite alone, let me tell you—and gaze around as if wondering where all the other birds *could* have gone to! And once in a while also a splendid white-headed eagle would come down out of the blue, and wing low over the barn, and scream his thin, terrifying yelp, as if he were hoping there might be something like spring lambs hidden in the barn. But none of these things, affairs of the garish, dazzling, common day, moved in the least the row of contented little bats, all drowsing the useless hours of day away as they hung by their toes in the soft gloom under the roof. They would wake up now and again, to be sure, and squeak, and crowd each other a little. Or perhaps rouse themselves enough to make a long and careful toilet, combing their exquisitely fine fur with their delicate claws, and passing every corner of the elastic silken membrane of their wings daintily between their lips. But as for what went on in the gaudy light on the outer side of the roof, it concerned them not at all.

But Little Silk Wing seems to have been born to illustrate the dangers which beset the life of the stay-at-home. For two days there had been an unwonted disturbance in the deep-grassed meadow that surrounded the barn. There had been the clanking of harness, the long, shrill, vibrant clatter of the scarlet mowing machine, the snorting of horses, and the shouting and laughter of men turning the fresh hay with their forks. Then came carts and children, with shrill laughter and screams of merriment, and the hay was hauled into the barn, load after load, fragrant, crackling with grasshoppers; and presently the mows began to fill up till the men with the pitchforks, sweating over the hot work of stowing the hay, came up beneath the eaves.

Reluctantly and indignantly the bats woke up. Some of them, as the loads came in with noisy children on top, bestirred themselves sufficiently to shake the sleep out of their eyes, unfold their draped wings, flutter down into the daylight, and fly off to the peaceful gloom of the nearest woods.

But the mother of Little Silk Wing was not so easily disturbed. She opened her tiny black beads of eyes as wide as she could, but gave no other sign of having noticed the invaders of the old barn's drowsy peace. She had seen such excitement before, and never known any harm to come of it. And she hated flying out into the full glare of the sun.

But there is such a thing, you know, as being a bit *too* calm and self-possessed. As the hay got higher up in the mow, beyond the eaves, and almost up to the level of the topmost beam, one of the farm hands noticed the little bat hanging under the ridgepole. He was one of those dull fools, not cruel at heart, perhaps, but utterly without imagination, who, if they see something interesting, are apt to kill it just because they don't know any other way to show their interest. He up with the handle of his pitchfork and knocked the poor little mother bat far out into the stubble."

"Oh!" cried the Child. "Didn't it hurt her *dreadfully?*"

"It killed her," replied Uncle Andy simply. "But by chance it didn't hurt Little Silk Wing himself, as he clung desperately to her neck. The children, with cries of sympathy and reprobation, rushed to pick up the little dark body. But the black-and-white dog was ahead of them. He raced in and snatched the queer thing up, gently enough, in his teeth. But he let it drop again at once in huge surprise. It had come apart. All of a sudden it was two bats instead of one. He couldn't understand it at all. And neither could the children. And while they stood staring—the black-and-white dog with his tongue hanging out and his tail forgetting to wag, and the children with their eyes quite round—Little Silk Wing fluttered up into the air, flew hesitatingly this way and that for a moment till he felt sure of himself, and then darted off to the shelter of those woods where he had so often accompanied his mother on her hunting."

The Child heaved a sigh of relief. "I'm so glad he got off," he murmured.

"I thought you would be. That's why he did," said Uncle Andy enigmatically.

CHAPTER IX

A LITTLE ALIEN IN THE WILDERNESS

It was too hot and clear and still that morning for the most expert of fishermen to cast his fly with any hope of success. The broad pale-green lily pads lay motionless on the unruffled breast of Silverwater. Nowhere even the round ripple of a rising minnow broke the blazing sheen of the lake. The air was so drowsy that those sparks of concentrated energy, the dragonflies, forgot to chase their aerial quarry and slept, blazing like amethysts, rubies and emeralds, on the tops of the cattail rushes. Very lazily and without the slightest reluctance, Uncle Andy ruled in his line, secured his cast, and leaned his rod securely in a forked branch to await more favorable conditions for his pet pastime. For the present it seemed to him that nothing could be more delightful and more appropriate to the hour than to lie under the thick-leaved maple at the top of the bank, and smoke and gaze out in lotus-eating mood across the enchanted radiance of the water. Even the Child, usually as restless as the dragonflies themselves or those exponents of perpetual motion, the brown water skippers, was lying on his back, quite still, and staring up with round, contemplative blue eyes through the diaphanous green of the maple leaves.

Though his eyes were so very wide open, it was that extreme but ephemeral openness which a child's eyes so frequently assume just before closing up very tight. In fact, in just about three-eights of a minute he would have been, in all probability, sound asleep, with a rose-pink light, sifted through his eyelids, dancing joyously over his dreams. But at that moment there came a strange cry from up the sweeping curve of the shore—so strange a cry that the Child sat up instantly very straight, and demanded, with a gasp, "What's that?"

Uncle Andy did not answer for a moment. Perhaps it was because he was so busy lighting his pipe, or perhaps he hoped to hear the sound again before committing himself—for so experienced a woodsman as he was had good reason to know that most of the creatures of the wild have many different cries, and sometimes seem to imitate each other in the strangest fashion. He had not long to wait. The wild voice sounded again and again, so insistently, so appealingly that the Child became greatly excited over it. The sound was something between the bleat of an extraordinary, harsh-voiced kid and the scream of a badly frightened mirganser, but more penetrating and more strident than either.

"Oh, it's frightened, Uncle Andy!" exclaimed the Child. "What do you think it is? What does it want? Let's go and see if we can't help it!"

The pipe was drawing all right now, because Uncle Andy had made up his mind.

"It's nothing but a young fawn—a baby deer," he answered. "Evidently it has got lost, and it's crying for its mother. With a voice like that it ought to make her hear if she's anywhere alive—if a bear has not jumped on her and broken her neck for her. Ah! there she comes," he added, as the agitated bellowing of a doe sounded from further back in the woods. The two cries answered each other at intervals for a couple of minutes, rapidly nearing. And then they were silent.

The Child heaved a sigh of relief.

"I'm so glad he found his mother again!" he murmured. "It must be terrible to be lost in the woods—to be *quite* alone, and not know, when you cried, whether it would be your mother or a bear that would come running to you from under the black trees!"

"I agree with you," said Uncle Andy, with unwonted heartiness. It was not too often that he was able to agree completely with the Child's suggestions in regard to the affairs of the wild. "Yes, indeed," he added reminiscently; "I tried it myself once, when I was about your age, away down in the Lower Ottanoonsis Valley, when the country thereabouts was not settled like it is now. And I didn't like it at all, let me tell you."

"What came?" demanded the Child breathlessly. "Was it your mother, or a bear?"

"Neither!" responded Uncle Andy. "It was Old Tom Saunders, Bill's uncle—only he wasn't old, or Bill's uncle, at that time, as you may imagine if you think about it."

"Oh!" said the Child, a little disappointed. He had rather hoped it was the bear, since he felt assured of his uncle's ultimate safety.

"And I knew a little Jersey calf once," continued Uncle Andy, being now fairly started in his reminiscences and unwilling to disappoint the Child's unfailing thirst for a story, "in the same woods, who thought she was lost when she wasn't, and made just as much noise over it as if she had been. That, you see, was what made all the trouble. She was a good deal of a fool at that time—which was not altogether to be wondered at, seeing that she was only one day old; and when her mother left her sleeping under a bush for a few minutes, while she went down through the swamp to get a drink at the brook a couple of hundred feet away, the little fool woke up and thought herself deserted. She set up such a bleating as was bound to cause something to happen in that wild neighborhood."

"Yes!" said the Child, almost in a whisper. "And which came *this* time—her mother or the bear?"

"Both!" replied Uncle Andy, most unexpectedly.

"Oh!" gasped the Child, opening his mouth till it was as round as his eyes. And for once he had not a single question ready.

"You see, it was this way," went on Uncle Andy, prudently giving him no time to think one up. "When the bear heard that noise he knew very well that the calf was all alone. And, being hungry, he lost no time in coming to seize the opportunity. What he didn't know was that the mother was so near. Naturally, he would never think the calf would make such a fuss if the mother were only down by the brook getting a drink. So he came along through the bushes at a run, taking no precautions whatever. And the mother came up from the brook at a run. And they met in a little open spot, about fifty feet from where the foolish calf stood, bawling under her bush. She stopped bawling and stood staring when she saw the bear and her mother meet.

The bear was a big one, very hungry, and savage at the slightest hint that his meal, right there in sight, was going to be interfered with. The mother was a little fawn-colored Jersey cow, with short, sharp horns pointing straight forward, and game to the last inch of her trim make-up. Her fury, at sight of that black hulk approaching her foolish young one, was nothing short of a madness. But it was not a blind madness. She knew what she was doing, and was not going to let rage lose her a single point in the game of life and death.

In spite of her disadvantage in being down the slope and so having to charge straight uphill, she hurled herself at the enemy with a ferocity that rather took him aback. He wheeled, settled upon his haunches, and lifted a massive forepaw, to meet the attack of a blow that should settle the affair at once. But the little cow was not to be caught so. Almost as the bear delivered his lunging stroke she checked herself, jumped aside with a nimbleness that no bull could have begun to match, and sank both horns deep into her great antagonist's flank. Before she could spring back again beyond his reach, however, with a harsh groan he swung about, and with the readiness of an accomplished boxer brought down his other forepaw across her neck, smashing the spine. Without a sound the gallant little cow crumpled up and fell in a heap against the bear's haunches.

Throwing her off violently, he struck her again and again, as if in a panic. Then, realizing that she was quite dead, he drew away, bit fiercely at the terrible wound in his flank, and dragged himself away, whimpering. For the time, at least, his appetite was quite gone.

Uncomprehending, but very anxious, the calf had watched the swift duel. The finish of it dismayed her, but, of course, she did not know why. She could only feel that, in spite of the disappearance of the bear, it was not altogether satisfactory. She had trembled instinctively at sight of the bear. And now, curiously enough, she trembled at the sight of her mother, lying there in a heap, so still."

Uncle Andy's way of putting it was somehow so vivid that the Child trembled too at that.

"After a while," continued Uncle Andy, "when she saw that her mother made no sign of rising and coming to her, she came staggering down from her place under the bush, her long, awkward legs very difficult to manage. Reaching her mother's side, she poked her coaxingly with her wet little muzzle. Meeting no response, she poked her impatiently, and even butted her. When even this brought no response, a sudden overwhelming terror chilled her heart, and her weak knees almost gave way. She had an impulse to run from this thing that looked like her mother and smelled like her mother, and yet was evidently, after all, *not* her mother. She was afraid to stay there. But she was also afraid to go away. And then she just began to bawl again at the top of her voice, for she was not only frightened and lonely, but also hungry.

"Of course, everything in the woods for half a mile around heard her bawling."

And just here Uncle Andy had the heartlessness to pause and relight his pipe.

"And then—another bear came!" broke in the Child breathlessly.

"No, not exactly," responded Uncle Andy at last. "Of course, lots of things came to see what all that queer noise was about—stealthy things, creeping up silently and peering with round bright eyes from thickets and weed tufts. But the calf did not see or notice any of these. All she saw was a tall, dark, ungainly looking, long-legged creature, half as tall again as her mother had been, with no horns, a long clumsy head, thick overhanging nose, and big splay hooves. She didn't quite know whether to be frightened at this great, dark form or not. But she stopped her noise, I can tell you.

"Well, the tall stranger stood still, about thirty or forty paces away, eyeing the calf with interest and the fawn-colored heap on the ground with suspicion. Then, all at once, the calf forgot her fears. She was so lonely, you know, and the stranger did not look at all like a bear. So, with a little appealing *Bah,* she ran forward clumsily, straight up to the tall stranger's side, paused a moment at the alien smell, and then, with a cool impudence only possible at the age of twenty-five hours, began to help herself to a dinner of fresh milk. The tall stranger turned her great dark head far around, sniffed doubtfully for a few seconds, and fell to licking the presumptuous one's back assiduously."

"I know," said the Child proudly. "It was a moose."

"I'd have been ashamed of you," said Uncle Andy, "if you hadn't known that at once from my description. Of course, it was a cow moose. But where the calf's great piece of luck came in was in the fact that the moose had lost *her* calf, just the day before, through its falling into the river and being swept away by the rapids. Her heart, heavy with grief and loneliness, her udder aching with the pressure of its milk, she had been drawn up to see what manner of baby it was that dared to cry its misery so openly here in the dangerous forest.

"And when the calf adopted her so confidently, after a brief shyness—the shyness of all wild things toward the creatures who have come under man's care—she returned the compliment of adopting the calf.

"After a little, when the calf had satisfied its appetite, she led it away through the trees. It followed readily enough for a while—for perhaps half a mile. Then it got tired, and stopped with its legs sprawled apart, and bawled after her appealingly. At first she seemed surprised at its tiring so soon. But with a resigned air she stopped. The calf at once lay down and resolutely went to sleep. Its wild mother, puzzled but patient, stood over it protectingly, licking its silky coat (so much softer than her own little one's had been), and smelling it all over as if unable to get used to the peculiar scent. When it woke up she led it on again, this time for perhaps a good mile before it began to protest against such incomprehensible activity. And so, by easy stages and with many stops, she led the little alien on, deep into her secret woods, and brought it, about sunset, to the shore of a tiny secluded lake.

"That same evening the farmer, looking for his strayed cow, came upon the dead body on the slope above the stream. He saw the marks of the fight and the tracks of the bear, and understood the story in part. But he took it for granted that the bear, after killing the mother, had completed the job by carrying off the calf. The tracks of the moose he paid no attention to, never dreaming that they concerned him in the least. But the bear he followed, vowing vengeance, till he lost the trail in the gathering dusk, and had to turn home in a rage, consoling himself with plans for bear traps.

"In her home by the lake, caressed and tenderly cared for by her tall new mother, the calf quickly forgot her real mother's fate. She forgot about the whole affair except for one thing. She remembered to be terribly afraid of bears—and that fear is indeed the beginning of wisdom, as far as all the children of the wild are concerned. She would start and tremble at sight of any particularly dense and bulky shadow, and to come unexpectedly upon a big black stump was for some weeks a painful experience. But the second step in wisdom—the value of silence—she was very slow to learn. If her new mother got out of her sight for half a minute she would begin bawling after her in a way that must have been a great trial to the nerves of a reticent, noiseless moose cow. The latter, moreover, could never get over the idea that to cause all that noise some dreadful danger must be threatening. She would come charging back on the run, her mane stiff on her back and her eyes glaring, and she would hunt every thicket in the neighborhood before she could feel quite reassured. Meanwhile, the calf would look with wonder in her big, velvet-soft eyes, with probably no slightest notion in her silly head as to what was making her new mother so excited."

"How inconvenient that they couldn't talk," exclaimed the Child, who had great faith in the virtue of explanations.

Uncle Andy rubbed his chin thoughtfully.

"I suppose," he said, after a pause, "that the wild creatures *do* talk among themselves, more or less and after a fashion. But, you see, such simple speech as the calf possessed was only what she had inherited, and that, of course, was cow language and naturally unintelligible to a moose. However, babies learn easily, and it was not long before she and her new mother understood each other pretty well on most points of importance.

"There were wildcats and foxes and a pair of big, tuft-eared, wild-eyed lynxes living about the lake, and these all came creeping up one after another, under the cover of the thickets, to stare in amazement at the alien little one so tenderly mothered by the great cow moose. They had seen calves, on the farms of the settlement, and they regarded this one not only with the greed of the hungry prowler, but with a particularly cruel hostility as one of the retainers of feared and hated Man. But for all their anger they took care not to thrust themselves upon the attention of the moose. They appreciated too well the fury of her mother wrath, the swiftness and deadliness of the stroke of her knife-edged forehooves. They were not going to let their curiosity obscure their discretion, you may be sure, like some of the childish deer and antelope often do."

"Why?" interrupted the Child eagerly, being all at once consumingly anxious to know what the deer and antelope were curious about. But Uncle Andy paid no attention whatever.

"Then, one morning," he continued, "two other moose cows came along up the lake shore, followed by their long-legged, shambling youngsters. They stopped to discuss the condition of lily roots with their tall sister; but at the sight of her nursing and petting and mothering a *calf*—a baby of the cattle tribe whom they despised and hated for its subservience to man and for living tamely behind fences, they became quite disagreeable. They sniffed loudly and superciliously. The calf, however, looking very small and neat and bright in her clean coat of fawn color beside the gaunt, awkward moose babies, was not in the least afraid of the disagreeable strangers. She pranced up boldly to investigate them.

"They wouldn't be investigated by the saucy little alien, and in a moment of folly one of them struck at her. The foster mother had been watching their attitude with jealous eyes and rising wrath, and now her wrath exploded. With a hoarse bleat she sprang upon the offender and sent her sprawling down the bank clean into the water. Then she turned upon the other. But this one, with quick discretion, was already trotting off hastily, followed by the two awkward youngsters. The triumphant foster mother turned to the calf and anxiously smelled it all over to make sure it had not been hurt. And the rash cow in the water, boiling with wrath, but afraid to risk a second encounter, picked herself up from among the lily pads and shambled off after her retreating party.

"As the summer deepened, however, the calf began to feel and act more like a moose calf—to go silently and even to absorb some of her foster mother's smell. The other moose began to get used to her, even quite to tolerate her; and the wild creatures generally ceased to regard her as anything but a very unusual kind of moose. Of course, she *thought* she *was* a moose. She grew strong, sleek and nimble-footed on her foster mother's abundant milk, and presently learned to browse on the tender leaves and twigs of the fresh green shrubbery. She soon, however, found that the short, sweet grasses of the forest glades were much more to her taste than any leaves or stringy twigs. But the lily roots which her foster mother taught her to pull from the muddy lake bottom, as they wallowed luxuriously side by side in the cool water, defying flies and heat, suited her admirably. The great black moose bulls—hornless at this season and fat and amiable as sheep—regarded her with a reserved curiosity; and the moose calves, the strangeness of her form and color once worn off, treated her with great respect. Though she was so much smaller and lighter than they, her quickness on her feet and her extremely handy way of butting made her easily master of them all. Even the supercilious young cow who had been so disagreeable to her at first grew indifferently friendly, and all was peace around the secluded little lake.

"Late one afternoon, however, when the shadows were getting long and black across the forest glades, the peace was momentarily broken. The calf was pasturing in one of the glades, while her foster mother was wallowing and splashing down among the lilies. A bear creeping up through the thickets so noiselessly that not even a sharp-eyed chick-a-dee or a vigilant red squirrel took alarm, peered out between the branches and saw the calf.

"As luck would have it, it was the same old bear! He had recovered from his wound, but naturally he had not forgotten the terrible horns of the little fawn-colored Jersey cow. When he saw the fawn-colored calf he flew into a rage, and hurled himself forth at her to avenge in one stroke the bitter and humiliating memory.

"But the calf was too quick for him. At the first crackling of the branches behind her she had jumped away like a deer. From the corner of her eye she saw the great black shape rushing upon her, and, with a wild cry, half the bawl of a calf, half the bleat of a young moose, she went racing, tail in air, down to the water, with the bear at her heels.

"With a terrific splashing the cow moose hurried to the rescue. She was a very big moose and she was in a very big rage; and very formidable she looked as she came plowing her way to shore, sending up the water in fountains before her. He knew well that a full-grown cow moose was an awkward antagonist to tackle when she was in earnest. This one seemed to him to be very much in earnest. He hesitated and stopped his rush when about halfway down the bank. Caution began to cool his vengeful humor. After all, it seemed there was really no luck for him in a fawn-colored calf. He'd try a red one or a black-and-white one next time. As he came to this conclusion, the indignant moose came to shore. Whereupon, he wheeled with a grunt and made off, just a little faster, perhaps, than was *quite* consistent with his dignity, into the darkness of the fir thickets. The moose, with the coarse hair standing up stiffly along her neck, shook herself and stood glaring after him.

"Through the summer and autumn the calf found it altogether delightful being a moose. As the cold began to bite her hair began to thicken up a protection against it; but, nevertheless, with her thin, delicate skin she felt it painfully. After the first heavy snowfall she had a lot of trouble to get food, having to paw down through the snow for every mouthful of withered grass. When the snow got to be three or four feet deep, and her foster mother, along with a wide-antlered bull, three other cows, and a couple of youngsters had trodden out a "moose yard" with its maze of winding alleys, her plight grew sore. All along the bottom edges of these alleys she nibbled the dead grass and dry herbage, and she tried to browse, like her companions, on the twigs of poplar and birch. But the insufficient, unnatural food and the sharp cold hit her hard. She would huddle up beneath her mother's belly or crowd down among the rest of the herd for warmth, but long before Christmas she had become a mere bag of bones."

The Child shivered sympathetically. But, remembering the Snowhouse Baby, he could not help inquiring:

"Why didn't she make herself a house in the snow?"

"Didn't know enough!" answered Uncle

Andy shortly. "Did you ever hear of any of the cow kind having sense enough for that? Well, it's a pretty sure thing, you may take it, that she would never have pulled through the winter if something unexpected hadn't happened to change her luck.

"It was the farmer—the one who had owned her mother, and who, of course, really owned her, too.

"With his hired man and a team of two powerful backwoods horses and a big sled for axes and food, he had come back into the woods to cut the heavy spruce timber which grew around the lake. A half-mile back from the lake, on the opposite shore, he had his snug log camp and his warm little barn full of hay. He and his man had everything they needed for their comfort except fresh meat. And when they came upon the winding paths of the 'moose yard' they knew they were not going to lack meat for long.

"On the following day, on snowshoes, the two men explored the 'yard,' tramping along beside the deep-trodden trails. Soon they came upon the herd, and marked the lofty antlers of the bull towering over a bunch of low fir bushes. The farmer raised his heavy rifle. It was an easy shot. He fired, and the antlered head went down.

"At the sound of the shot and the fall of their trusted leader, the herd scattered in panic, breasting down the walls of their paths and floundering off through the deep snow. The two men stared after them with interest, but made no motion for another shot, for it was against the New Brunswick law to kill a cow moose, and if the farmer had indulged himself in such a luxury it would have cost him a hundred pounds by way of a fine.

"Among the fleeing herd appeared a little fawn-colored beast, utterly unlike any moose calf that the farmer or his man had ever heard of. It was tremendously nimble at first, bouncing along at such a rate that it was impossible to get a really good look at it. But its legs were much too short for such a depth of snow, and before it had gone fifty yards it was quite used up. It stopped, floundered on another couple of yards, and then lay down quite helplessly. The two men hurried up. It turned upon them a pair of large, melting, velvet eyes—frightened, indeed, but not with that hopeless, desperate terror that comes to the eyes of the wild creatures when they are trapped.

"'Well, I'll be jiggered if that ain't old Blossom's calf that we made sure the bear had carried off!' cried the farmer, striding up and gently patting the calf's ribs. 'My, but you're poor!' he went on. 'They hain't used yer right out here in the woods, have they? I reckon ye'll be a sight happier back home in the old barn.'"

Uncle Andy knocked the ashes out of his pipe and stuck it back in his pocket.

"That's all!" said he, seeing that the Child still looked expectant.

"But," protested the Child, "I want to know——"

"Now, you know very well all the rest," said Uncle Andy. "What's the use of my telling you how the calf was taken back to the settlement, and got fat, and grew up to give rich milk like cream, as every good Jersey should? You can think all that out for yourself, you know."

"But the moose cow," persisted the Child. "Didn't she feel *dreadful?*"

"Well," agreed Uncle Andy, "perhaps she did. But don't you go worrying about that. She got over it. The next spring she had another calf, a real moose calf, to look after, you know."

CHAPTER X

WHAT HE SAW WHEN HE KEPT STILL

The Child was beginning to feel that if he could not move very soon he'd burst.

Of course, under Uncle Andy's precise instructions he had settled himself in the most comfortable position possible before starting upon the tremendous undertaking of keeping perfectly still for a long time. To hold oneself perfectly still and to keep the position as tirelessly as the most patient of the wild creatures themselves—this, he had been taught by Uncle Andy, was one of the first essentials to the acquirement of true woodcraft, as only such stillness and such patience could admit one to anything like a real view of the secrets of the wild. Even the least shy of the wilderness folk are averse to going about their private and personal affairs under the eyes of strangers, and what the Child aspired to was the knowledge of how to catch them off their guard. He would learn to see for himself how the rabbits and the partridges, the woodchucks and the weasels, the red deer, the porcupines, and all the other furtive folk who had their habitations around the tranquil shores of Silverwater, were really accustomed to behave themselves when they felt quite sure no one was looking.

Before consenting to the Child's initiation, Uncle Andy had impressed upon him with the greatest care the enormity of breaking the spell of stillness by even the slightest and most innocent-seeming movement.

"You see," had said Uncle Andy, "it's this way! When we get to the place where we are going to hide and watch, you may think that we're quite alone. But not so. From almost every bush, from surely every thicket, there'll be at least one pair of bright eyes staring at us—maybe several pairs. They'll be wondering what we've come for; they'll be disliking us for being so clumsy and making such a racket, and they'll be keeping just as still as so many stones in the hope that we won't see them—except, of course, certain of the birds, which fly in the open and are used to being seen, and don't care a hang for us because they think us such poor creatures in not being able to fly——"

At this point the Child had interrupted:

"Wouldn't they be surprised," he murmured, "if we did?"

"I expect they've got some surprises coming to them that way one of these days!" agreed Uncle Andy. "But, as I was saying, we'll be well watched ourselves for a while. But it's a curious thing about the wild creatures, or at least about a great many of them, that for all their keenness their eyes don't seem to *distinguish* things as sharply as we do. The very slightest movement they detect, sometimes at an astonishing distance. But when a person is perfectly motionless for a long time, they seem to confuse him with the stumps and stones and bushes in a most amazing fashion. Perhaps it is that the eyes of some of them have not as high a power of differentiation as ours. Perhaps it is that when a fellow is a long time still they think he's dead. We'll have to let the scientists work that out for us. But if you go on the way you're beginning (and I'm bound to say you're doing very well indeed, considering that you're not *very* big), you'll often have occasion to observe that some of the wild creatures, otherwise no fools, are more afraid of a bit of colored rag fluttering in the wind than of an able-bodied man who sits staring right at them, if only he doesn't stir a finger. But only let him wiggle that finger, his very littlest one, and off they'll be."

The Child put his hand behind his back and wiggled his little finger gently, smiling to think what sharp eyes it would take to see *that* motion. But his Uncle, as if divining his thoughts, went on to say:

"It's not as if those sly, shy watchers were all in front of you, you know. The suspicious eyes will be all around you. Perhaps it may be a tiny wood-mouse peering from under a root two or three steps behind you. You have been perfectly still, say, for ten minutes, and the mouse is just beginning to think that you *may* be something quite harmless. She rubs her whiskers, and is just about to come out when, as likely as not, you move your fingers a little, behind your back"—here the Child blushed guiltily, and thrust both his grimy little fists well to the front—"feeling quite safe because *you* don't see the movement yourself.

"Well, the mouse sees it. She realizes at once that you aren't dead, after all—in fact, that you're a dangerous deceiver. She wisks indignantly back into her hole. Somebody else sees her alarm, and follows her example, and in two seconds it's gone all about the place that you're not a stump or a stone or a harmless dead thing waiting to be nibbled at, but a terrible enemy lying in wait for them all. So you see how important it is to keep still, with the real stillness of dead things."

The Child winked his eyes rapidly. "But I can't keep from *winking,* Uncle Andy," he protested. "I'll promise not to wiggle my fingers or wrinkle my nose. But if I don't wink my eyes sometimes they'll begin to smart and get full of tears, and then I won't be able to see anything—and then all the keeping still will be just wasted."

"Of course, you won't be able to keep from winking," agreed Uncle Andy. "And, of course, you won't be able to keep from *breathing.* But you mustn't make a noise about either process."

"How can I make a noise winking?" demanded the Child in a voice of eager surprise. If such a thing were possible he wanted to learn how at once.

"Oh, nonsense!" returned Uncle Andy. "Now, listen to me! We're nearly there, and I don't want to have to do any more talking, because the quieter we are now the sooner the wild folk will get over their first suspiciousness. Now, after we once get fixed, you won't move a muscle, not even if two or three mosquitoes alight on you at once and begin to help themselves?"

"No!" agreed the Child confidently. He was accustomed to letting mosquitoes bite him, just for the fun of seeing their gray, scrawny bodies swell up and redden till they looked like rubies.

"Well, we'll hope there won't be any mosquitoes!" said Uncle Andy reassuringly. "And if a yellow-jacket lights on your sock and starts to crawl up under the leg of your knickers, you won't stir?"

"N-no!" agreed the Child, with somewhat less confidence. He had had such an experience before, and remembered it with a pang. Then he remembered that he had enough string in his pockets to tie up both legs so securely that not the most enterprising of wasps could get under. His confidence returned. "No, Uncle Andy!" he repeated, with earnest resolution.

"Umph! We'll see," grunted Uncle Andy doubtfully, not guessing what the Child had in mind. But when he saw him, with serious face, fish two bits of string from the miscellaneous museum of his pocket and proceed to frustrate the problematical yellow-jacket he grinned appreciatively.

The place for the watching had been well chosen by Uncle Andy—a big log to lean their backs against, a cushion of deep, dry moss to sit upon, and a tiny, leafy sapling of silver poplar twinkling its light-hung leaves just before their faces, to screen them a little without interfering with their view. Their legs, to be sure, stuck out beyond the screen of the poplar sapling, in plain sight of every forest wayfarer. But legs were of little consequence so long as they were not allowed to kick.

For just about a minute the Child found it easy to keep still. In the second minute his nose itched, and he began to wonder how long they had been there. In the third minute he realized that there was a hard little stick in the moss that he was sitting on. In the fourth minute it became a big stick, and terribly sharp, so that he began to wonder if it would pierce right through him and make him a cripple for life. He feared that perhaps Uncle Andy had never thought of a danger like this, and he felt that he ought to call attention to it. But before he had quite made up his mind to such a desperate measure the fifth minute came—and with it the yellow-and-black wasp, which made the Child forget all about the stick in the moss. The wasp alighted on the red, mosquito-bitten, naked skin above the top of the Child's sock, and then, sure enough, started to go exploring up under the leg of his knickers. The Child felt nervous for a moment—and then triumphant. He just saved himself from laughing out loud at the thought of how he had fooled the inquisitive insect.

And so passed the fifth and sixth minutes. The seventh and eighth were absorbed in bitter doubts of Uncle Andy. The Child felt quite sure that he had been quite still for at least an hour. If nothing interesting had happened in all that time, then nothing interesting was going to happen, nothing interesting could happen. An awful distrust assailed him. Was it possible that Uncle Andy had merely adopted this base means of teaching him to keep still? Was it possible that even now Uncle Andy (whose face was turned the other way) was either laughing deeply in his sleeve or sleeping the undeservedly peaceful sleep of the successful deceiver?

To do the Child justice, he felt ashamed of such doubts as soon as he had fairly confronted himself with them. Then, in the ninth minute, both legs began to fill up with pins and needles. This occupied his attention. It was an axiom with him that under such painful conditions one should at once get up and move around. Placed thus between two directly conflicting duties, his conscience was torn. Then he remembered his promise. His grit was good, and he determined to keep his promise at all costs, no matter at what fatal consequence to his legs. And he derived considerable comfort from the thought that, if his leg should never be any use any more, his Uncle Andy would at least be stricken with remorse.

Then, as the tenth minute dragged its enormous, trailing length along, came that terrible feeling already alluded to—that he must either move or burst. With poignant self-pity he argued the two desperate alternatives within his soul. But, fortunately for him, before he felt himself obliged to come to any final decision, something happened, and his pain and doubts were forgotten.

Two big yellow-gray snowshoe rabbits came hopping lazily past, one just ahead of the other. One jumped clean over Uncle Andy's outstretched feet, as if they were of no account or interest whatever to a rabbit. The other stopped and thumped vigorously on the ground with his strong hind foot. At this signal the first one also stopped. They both sat up on their haunches, ears thrust forward in intense interrogation, and gazed at the two moveless figures behind the poplar sapling.

The one immediately in front of him absorbed all the Child's attention. Its great, bulging eyes surveyed him from head to foot, at first with some alarm, then with half-contemptuous curiosity. Its immensely long ears see-sawed meditatively, and its queer three-cornered mouth twinkled incessantly as if it were talking to itself. At last, apparently having decided that the Child was nothing worth taking further notice of, it dropped on all fours, nibbled at a leaf, discarded it, and hopped off to find more tasty provender. Its companion, having "sized up" Uncle Andy in the same way, presently followed. But being of the more suspicious disposition, it stopped from time to time to glance back and assure itself that the strange, motionless things behind the poplar sapling were not attempting to follow it.

The Child was immensely interested. He thought of a lot of questions to ask as soon as he should be allowed to speak, and he resolved to remember every one of them. But just as he was getting them arranged a small, low, long-bodied, snaky-slim, yellowish beast came gliding by and drove them all clean out of his head. It was a weasel. It almost bumped into the Child's feet before it noticed them. Then it jumped back, showing its keen teeth in a soundless snarl of its narrow, pointed muzzle, and surveyed the Child with the cruellest little eyes that he had ever even imagined. The savage eyes stared him full in the face, a red light like a deep-buried spark coming into them, till he thought the creature was going to spring at his throat. Then gradually the spark died out, as the little furry reassured itself. The triangular face turned aside. The working, restless nose sniffed sharply, catching the fresh scent of the two rabbits, and in the next instant the creature was off, in long, noiseless bounds, upon the hot trail. The Child knew enough of woodcraft to realize at once the meaning of its sudden departure, and he murmured sympathetically in his heart, "Oh, I do hope he won't catch them!"

All thoughts of the weasel and the rabbits, however, were speedily driven from his mind, for at this moment he noticed a fat, yellowish grub, with a chestnut-colored head, crawling up his sleeve. He hated grubs, and wondered anxiously if it had any unpleasant design of crawling down his neck. He squirmed inwardly at the idea. But just as he was coming to the conclusion that *that* was something he'd *never* be able to stand, a most unexpected ally came to his rescue. With a blow that *almost* made him jump out of his jacket, something lit on the fat grub. It was a big black hornet, with white bands across its shining body. She gave the grup a tiny prick with the tip of her envenomed sting, which caused it to roll up into a tight ball and lie still. Then straddling it, and holding it in place with her front pair of legs, she cut into it with her powerful mandibles and began to suck its juices. The Child's nose wrinkled in spite of himself at sight of this unalluring banquet, but he stared with all eyes. There was something terrifying to him in the swiftness and efficiency of the great hornet. Presently the grub, not having received quite a big enough dose of its captor's anæsthetic, came to under the devouring jaws and began to lash out convulsively. Another touch of the medicine in the hornet's tail, however, promptly put a stop to that, and once more it tightened up into an unresisting ball. Then straddling it again firmly, and handling it cleverly with its front legs as a raccoon might handle a big apple, she bit into it here and there, sucking eagerly with a quick, pumping motion of her body. The fat ball got smaller and smaller, till soon it was very little bigger than an ordinary sweet pea. The hornet turned it over and over impatiently, to see if anything more was to be got out of it; then she spurned it aside, and bounced into the air with a deep hum. She had certainly been very amusing, but the Child drew a breath of relief when she was gone. He had caught the copper-red flicker of her sting, as it barely touched the victim, and it seemed to him like a jet of live flame.

When the hornet was gone the Child began once more to remember that little stick in the soft moss beneath him. How had he ever forgotten it? He decided that he must have been sitting on it for hours and hours. But just as it was beginning fairly to burn its way into his flesh, a queer little rushing sound close at his side brought his heart into his throat. It was such a vicious, menacing little sound. Glancing down, he saw that a tiny wood-mouse had darted upon a big brown-winged butterfly and captured it. The big wings flapped pathetically for a few seconds; but the mouse bit them off, to save herself the bother of lagging useless material home to her burrow. She was so near that the Child could have touched her by reaching out his hand. But she took no more notice of him than if he had been a rotten stump. Less, in fact, for she might have tried to gnaw into him if he had been a rotten stump, in the hope of finding some wood-grubs.

The mouse dragged away the velvety body of the butterfly to her hole under the roots. She was no more than just in time, for no sooner was she out of sight than along came a fierce-eyed little shrew-mouse, the most audacious and pugnacious of the mouse tribe, who would undoubtedly have robbed her of her prey, and perhaps made a meal of her at the same time. He nosed at the wings of the butterfly, nibbled at them, decided they were no good, and then came ambling over to the Child's feet. Shoe-leather! That was something quite new to him. He nibbled at it, didn't seem to think much of it, crept along up to the top of the shoe, sniffed at the sock, and came at last plump upon the Child's bare leg. "Was he going to try a nibble at that, too?" wondered the Child anxiously, his blue eyes getting very big and round. But no. This live, human flesh—*unmistakably* alive—and the startling Man smell of it, were too much for the nerves of his shrewship. With a squeak of indignation and alarm he sprang backward and scurried off among the weed-stalks.

"*There,* now!" thought the Child, in intense vexation. "He's gone and given the alarm!" But, as good luck would have it, he had done nothing of the kind. For a red fox, trotting past just then at a distance of not more than ten or a dozen feet, served to all observers as a more than ample explanation of the shrew's abrupt departure. The fox turned his head at the sound of the scurry and squeak, and very naturally attributed it to his own appearance on the scene. But at the same time he caught sight of those two motionless human shapes sitting rigid behind the poplar sapling. They were so near that his nerves received a shock. He jumped about ten feet; and then, recovering himself with immense self-possession, he sat up on his haunches to investigate. Of course, he was quite familiar with human beings and their ways, and he knew that they never kept still in that unnatural fashion unless they were either asleep or dead. After a searching scrutiny—head sagely to one side and mouth engagingly half open—he decided that they might be either dead or asleep, whichever they chose, for all he cared. He rose to his feet and trotted off with great deliberation, leaving on the still air a faint, half-musky odor which the Child's nostrils were keen enough to detect. As he went a bluejay which had been sitting on the top of a near-by tree caught sight of him, darted down, and flew along after him, uttering harsh screeches of warning to the rest of the small folk of the wilderness. It is not pleasant even in the wilderness to have "Stop thief! Stop thief! Thief! Thief! Thief!" screeched after you by a bluejay. And the fox glanced up at the noisy bird as if he would have been ready to give two fat geese and a whole litter of rabbits for the pleasure of crunching her impudent neck.

All this while there had been other birds in view besides the bluejay—chick-a-dees and nut-hatches hunting their tiny prey among the dark branches of the fir-trees, Canada sparrows fluting their clear call from the tree tops, flycatchers darting and tumbling in their zigzag, erratic flights, and sometimes a big goldenwing woodpecker running up and down a tall, dead trunk which stood close by, and *rat-tat-*

tat-tatting in a most businesslike and determined manner. But the Child was not, as a rule, so interested in birds as in the four-footed kindreds. Just now, however, a bird came on the scene which interested him extremely. It was a birch-partridge (or ruffled grouse) hen, accompanied by a big brood of her tiny, nimble chicks. They looked no bigger than chestnuts as they swarmed about her, crowding to snatch the dainties which she kept turning up for them. The Child watched them with fascinated eyes, not understanding how things so tiny and so frail as these chicks could be so amazingly quick and strong in their movements. Suddenly, at a little distance through the bushes, he caught sight of the red fox coming back, with an air of having forgotten something. The Child longed to warn the little partridge mother, but, realizing that he must not, he waited with thumping heart for a tragedy to be enacted before him.

He had no need to worry, however. The little mother saw the fox before he caught sight of her. The Child saw her stiffen herself suddenly, with a low *chit* of warning which sounded as if it might have come from anywhere. On the instant every chick had vanished. The Child realized that it was impossible for even such active creatures as they were to have run away so quickly as all that. So he knew that they had just made themselves invisible by squatting absolutely motionless among the twigs and moss which they so exactly resembled in coloring.

The fox, meanwhile, had been gazing around in every direction but the right one, to try and see where that partridge cry had come from. He liked partridge, and it was some time since he had had any. All at once he was surprised and pleased to see a hen partridge, apparently badly wounded, drop fluttering on the moss almost under his nose. He sprang forward to seize her, but she managed to flutter feebly out of his reach. It was obviously her last effort, and he was not in the least discouraged. She proved, however, to have many such last efforts, and the last the Child saw of the fox he was still hopefully jumping at her, as he disappeared from view among the underbrush. About three minutes later there was a hard *whirr* of wings, and the triumphant little mother reappeared. She alighted on the very spot whence she had first caught sight of the fox, stood for a moment stiffly erect, while she stared about her with keen, bright eyes, and then she gave a soft little call. Instantly the chicks were all about her, apparently springing up out of the ground as at the utterance of a spell. And proudly she led them away to another feeding ground.

What more the Child might have seen had time been allowed him will never be known, for now the session was interrupted. He was hoping for a porcupine to come by, or a deer, or a moose. He was half-hoping, half-fearing that it might be a bear, or a big Canadian lynx with dreadful eyes and tufted ears. But before any of these more formidable wonders arrived he heard a sound of rushing—of eager, desperate flight. Then a rabbit came into view—he felt sure it was one of the two who appeared at the beginning of his watch. The poor beast was plainly in an ecstasy of terror, running violently, but as it were aimlessly, and every now and then stopping short, all of a-tremble, as if despair were robbing it of its powers. It ran straight past the poplar sapling, swerved off to the right, and disappeared;

but the Child could hear the sound of its going and perceived that it was making a circle. A couple of seconds later came the weasel, running with its nose in the air, as if catching the scent from the air rather than from the fugitive's tracks.

The weasel did not seem to be in any hurry at all. It was the picture of cool, deadly, implacable determination. And the Child hated it savagely. Just opposite the poplar sapling it paused, seeming to listen. Then it bounded into the bushes on a short circle, saving itself unnecessary effort, as if it had accurately estimated the tactics of its panic-stricken quarry. A few moments later the rabbit reappeared, running frantically. Just as it came once more before the poplar sapling—not more than a couple of yards from the Child's feet, out from under a neighboring bush sprang the weasel, confronting it fairly. With a scream the rabbit stopped short and crouched in its tracks, quivering, to receive its doom.

The weasel leaped straight at its victim's throat. But it never arrived. For at that moment the Child gave vent to a shrill yell of indignation and jumped at the slayer with hands, eyes and mouth wide open. He made such a picture that Uncle Andy exploded. The astonished weasel vanished. The rabbit, shocked back into its senses, vanished also, but in another direction. And the Child, pulling himself together, turned to his uncle with a very red face.

"I'm sorry!" he said sheepishly. "I'm *so* sorry, Uncle Andy. But I just *couldn't* help it. I didn't think."

"Oh, well!" said Uncle Andy, getting up and stretching, and rubbing his stiffened legs tenderly. "I can't say that I blame you I came mighty near doing the same thing myself when that fool of a rabbit squealed."

CHAPTER XI

THE LITTLE VILLAGER AND HIS UNFRIENDLY GUESTS

ACROSS the still surface of Silverwater, a gleam in the amber and violet dusk, came a deep booming call, hollow and melancholy and indescribably wild. *Tooh-hoo-oo-whooh-ooh-oo,* and again *whooh-ooh-ooh-oo,* it sounded; and though the evening was warm the Child gave a little shiver of delicious awe, as he always did when he heard the sunset summons of the great horned owl.

"That's a bad fellow for you, the Big Horned Owl," growled Uncle Andy. "He's worse than a weasel, and that's a hard thing to say about any of the wild folk. He's everybody's enemy, and always ready to kill much more than he can eat."

"*Some* owls aren't bad," suggested the Child. He had a soft spot in his heart for owls, because they were so downy, and had such round faces and such round eyes, and looked as if they thought of such wonderful, mysterious things which they would never tell.

"How do you know that?" demanded Uncle Andy suspiciously. "Mind, I'm not saying offhand that it isn't so, but I'd like to know where you get your information."

"Bill told me," said the Child, with more confidence in his tones than he usually accorded to this authority.

"Oh, Bill!" sniffed Uncle Andy. "And haven't you got used to Billy's fairy stories yet?"

There was an obstinate look in the Child's earnest blue eyes which showed that this time the imaginative guide had told him a tale which he was unwilling to discredit.

"I know very well, Uncle Andy," said he with a judicial air, "that Bill loves to yarn, and often pretends to know a lot of things that aren't so. But I think he's telling the truth this time. He said he was. It's a little owl that lives out West on the big sandy plains. And it makes its nest in holes on the ground. It knows how to dig these holes itself, you know; but it can't dig them half, or a quarter, so well as the prairie dogs can. So it gets the prairie dogs to let it live in their big, comfortable burrows; and in return for this hospitality it kills and eats some of the rattlesnakes, the very small ones, I suppose, of course, which come round among the burrows looking for the young prairie dogs. Well, you know, Uncle Andy, Bill has been out West himself, and he's seen the villages of the prairie dogs, and the little owls sitting on the tops of the hillocks which are on the roofs of the prairie dogs' houses, and the rattlesnakes coiled up here and there in the hot, sunny hollows. There were lots and lots of the prairie dogs, *millions* and millions of them, Bill said."

"There'd have been still more if it hadn't been for the little owls," said Uncle Andy with a grin. But seeing a grieved look on the Child's face, and remembering that he himself was none too fond of having his narratives broken in upon, he hastened to add politely, but pointedly, "I beg your pardon for interrupting. Please go on!"

"Well, as I was going to say," continued the Child, in quite his Uncle's manner, "Bill saw—he saw them himself, with his own eyes

—these millions and thousands of prairie dogs, and quite a lot of the little owls, and only just a very few of the rattlesnakes. So, you see, it looks as if the owls must have eaten some of the snakes, and, anyhow, I think Bill was telling the truth *this* time."

"Well," said Uncle after puffing at his pipe for a few complimentary moments of reflection, "there's one important thing which Bill appears to have neglected. He doesn't seem to have inquired the views of the prairie dogs on the subject. Now, if he'd got *their* opinion——"

"But how *could* he?" protested the Child reproachfully. He was always troubled when Uncle Andy displayed anything like a frivolous strain.

"To be sure! To be sure! You *couldn't* have expected that of Bill," agreed Uncle Andy. "Still, you know, the opinion of the prairie dogs would have been interesting, wouldn't it? Well, I'll tell you a story just as soon as I can get this old pipe to draw properly, and then you can judge the opinion of the prairie dogs as to whether the Little Burrowing Owl is 'good' or not. If their opinion does not agree with Bill's, why you can choose for yourself between the two.

"Prairie Dog Village was of considerable size, covering at it did perhaps a dozen acres of the dry, light prairie soil. Its houses were crowded together without any regard to order or arrangement, and so closely as to suggest that their owners imagined land was scarce in the neighborhood. It wasn't. For hundreds of miles in every direction the plains stretched away to the dim horizon. There was room everywhere, nothing much, in fact, *but* room, with a little coarse grass and plenty of clear air. But the population went in for crowding by preference, and didn't care a cactus whether it was hygienic or not.

"The houses were all underground, each with a rounded hillock of earth beside its front door; and the size of these hillocks was an indication of the size of the houses beneath, for they were all formed by the earth brought to the surface in the process of excavating the rooms and passages. On the tops of these hillocks the owners sat up in the sun to bark and chatter and gossip with their nearest neighbors, always ready to dive headlong down their front doors, with a twinkling of their hind feet, at the approach of danger.

"But if the village was large, the Little Villager himself was decidedly small. Some twelve or fifteen inches in length from the tip of his innocent-looking nose to the end of his short and quite undistinguished-looking tail, he seldom had occasion to stretch himself out to his full length, and therefore he seldom got the credit of such inches as he actually possessed. His ears were short and rounded, his eyes were large, softly bright, and as innocent-looking as his nose. His body was plump and rounded, and he looked almost as much a baby when quite grown up as he had looked when he was still a responsibility to his talkative little mother. In color he was of a grayish-brown on top, and of a dingy white underneath, with a black tip to his tail to give a finish which his costume would otherwise have lacked.

"Except for unimportant variations in size, there was perhaps some hundreds of thousands of others, just like the Little Villager, sitting on their hillocks, or popping in and out of their round doorways, and chattering and barking in shrill chorus under the pale blue dome of a lovely sky. But on the hillock next door to the Little Villager sat no garrulous, furry gossip like himself. That mould top was deserted. But at its foot, curled up and basking in the still blaze of the sun, close beside the doorway, lay a thick-bodied, dusty-colored rattler, the intricate markings on his back dimmed as if by too much light and heat. His venomous, triangular head, with the heavy jaw base that showed great poison pockets, lay flat on his coils, and he had the lazy, well-fed appearance of one who does not have to forage for his meals. Here and there, scattered at wide intervals throughout the village, were to be seen other rattlers, of all sizes, from foot-long youngsters up to stout fellows over a yard in length, either basking in the hollows or lazily wriggling their way between the hillocks. They seemed to pay no attention whatever to the furry villagers; for a rattler likes to make a huge meal when he's about it, and therefore does not bother often about the, to him, rather laborious process of dining. The villagers, on their part, also seemed to pay little attention to the snakes; except that those who chanced to be foraging on the coarse herbage which grew between the hillocks always got out of the way with alacrity if a wriggling form approached, and not one of the coiled baskers ever woke up and shifted its position but that a hundred pairs of bright, innocent eyes would be fixed upon it until its intentions became quite clear.

"The Little Villager, who had just come out of his burrow, sat straight up on his hindquarters, on the top of his hillock, with his forepaws hanging meekly over his breast, and glared all about him to see if any danger was in sight. The big rattler beside the door of the next hillock underwent his careful scrutiny, which convinced him that the reptile had recently made a good meal, and would not be dangerous until he had slept it off. Then he glanced skyward. A great hawk was winging its way up from the southern horizon, almost invisible in the strong, direct glare, but the Little Villager's keen eyes detected it. He barked a warning, and the sharp signal went around from hillock to hillock; and in half a minute all the big, babyish eyes were fixed upon the approach of the skying marauder. Everybody chattered about it shrilly till the hawk was straight over the village. Then suddenly the noise was hushed. The great bird half folded its wings and swooped, the air making a hissing hum in its rigid pinion tips. The swoop was lightning swift, but even swifter was the disappearance of the Little Villager, and of all his neighbors for fifty feet about him. Before the hawk reached earth they had dropped into their burrows.

"Checking himself abruptly, the hawk flew on over the tops of the hillocks, making unexpected zigzag rushes to right and left. But wherever he went, there the villagers had vanished, almost as if the wind of his approach had whisked them away. Baffled and indignant, he at last gave up the hope of a dinner of prairie dog, and dropped on a small rattler which was too sluggish from overeating to have noticed that there was any particular excitement in the village. Gripping the reptile in inexorable talons just behind its head, the great bird bit its backbone through, carried it to the nearest hillock, and proceeded to tear it to pieces. Calmly he made his meal, glancing around with eyes glassy hard and fiercely arrogant, while from every burrow in the neighborhood round, innocent heads peered forth, barking insult and defiance. They were willing enough that the rattler should be destroyed, but they wished the hawk to understand that his continued presence in the villages was not desired. Of the two foes, they preferred the rattler, to whose methods of administering fate they had grown so accustomed that they could regard them with something like philosophy, especially where only a neighborhood was concerned. But the hawk's attack was so abrupt and violent as to be upsetting to the nerves of the whole village.

"When the hawk had finished his meal and wiped his beak on the hard earth he flew off; and long before he was out of sight all the furry householders were out on top of their hillocks and chattering at the tops of their voices about the affair. The Little Villager himself, having been first to give the alarm, was particularly excited and important. But even he managed to calm himself down after a while. And then, feeling hungry from excess of emotion, he descended from his hillock and fell to nibbling grass stems.

"He had been but a few minutes at this engrossing occupation when from the door of a nearby burrow popped suddenly a small brown owl. The bird appeared with a haste which seemed to ruffle its dignity considerably. It was followed at once by its mate. The two blinked in the strong light, and turned to peer down the hole from which they emerged, as if expecting to be followed. They were snapping their strong hooked beaks like castanets, and hissing indignantly. But nothing more came out of the hole. They glared about them for several minutes with their immense, round, fiercely bright eyes. Then, lifting themselves like blown thistledown, with one waft of their broad, downy wings they floated over to the door of the Little Villager's burrow. They looked at it. They looked at the Little Villager where he sat holding a half-nibbled grass stone between his paws. They snapped their beaks once more, with angry decision, and with two or three awkward, scuttling steps, like a parrot walking on the floor of his cage, they plunged down, quite uninvited, into the burrow.

"The Little Villager sat just where he was for perhaps half a minute, barking with indignation. Then he followed the impertinent visitors. As he entered he heard a confused sound of shrill, angry chattering, explosive hissing, and savage snapping of beaks. Being able to see quite comfortably in the gloom, he distinguished his companion, the lady villager who was at that time occupying the burrow with him, doing her best to make the visitors understand that they were not welcome. Her language might have seemed clear enough. She made little rushes at them with open mouth and gnashing teeth, and her tones were just as unpleasant as she knew how to make them. But the guests confronted her with claws and beaks so ready and so formidable that she did not like to come to close quarters.

"Nor, indeed, when the Little Villager himself arrived was the situation very much altered. One of the owls turned and faced him, whereupon he, too, lost his resolution and confined himself to threats. The two owls, for their part, seemed to consider it wise to stand n the defensive rather than to force a battle ɔ a finish with their unwilling hosts. For ome minutes, therefore, the war of threats nd bad language went on, without fur or eathers actually flying. Then at last the Little 'illager, who was by nature an easy-going, nresentful soul, chanced to glance aside from is adversary; and it flashed into his mind ıat, after all, there was some room to spare ı the burrow. Anyhow, he was tired of the rgument. He turned away indifferently and egan to nibble at some tough grass stems 'hich he had brought down in case of a rainy ay. Seeing him thus yield the point at issue, is mate was not going to fight it out alone. he, too, turned her back with ostentatious in-ifference upon her rude guests, and went out nd sat on the top of the hillock to let her feel-ıgs calm down. The pair of owls, well satis-ed to have forced themselves upon the Little 'illager's hospitality, huddled together in their wn corner, and resumed the nap which had een so unpleasantly interrupted in their pre-ious residence."

"What was it that interrupted?" broke in ıe Child, glad that it was not *he* that could be accused of it, *that* time. "What was it that drove them out of their own burrow in such a hurry?"

"It was a big rattlesnake," answered Uncle Andy, quite politely, remembering that he himself had recently been guilty of an interruption. "I ought to have explained that before, but I was interested in the Little Villager and forgot it. It was a big rattlesnake which had got tired of its old hole and taken a fancy to that of the owls. So the owls had had nothing to do but get out, without even a half-minute to talk over the matter. And hating to stay out in the full glare of the sun, which was very hard on their eyes, they had invited themselves to live with the Little Villager just because his house was the first they came to.

"All the rest of the day the Little Villager and his companion were extremely discontented. Their burrow was a very roomy and comfortable one, but it was spoiled for them by the presence of those two moon-eyed, hook-beaked, solemn persons sitting side by side in the opposite corner. So they spent most of their time outside on the hillock, gossiping about it to their neighbors, who were extremely nterested and full of suggestions, but showed o inclination whatever to come and help turn he intruders out. That was a thing which ad never been attempted in their village, and he prairie dogs were not noted for their initi-tive. In learning to get together and live in illages they had apparently exhausted it all. They were always ready to chatter, from norning to night, about anything, and pro-est against it, and declare that it must not be ermitted, but they always shirked the bother f united action, even to suppress the most langerous and destructive of nuisances.

"When evening came, however, they had the ouse to themselves. The owls, getting lively s the sunset colors faded from the sky, cuttled forth and sat up side by side on the op of the hillock. As soon as it was full night, nd the stars had come out clear and large in he deeply crystalline sky, they began hovering ither and thither on their wide, soundless wings, hunting the tiny prairie mice, which swarmed among the hillocks after dark.

"While they were thus pleasantly occupied, the Little Villager and his companion had an idea. It was not a very usual thing with them, and they hastened to act upon it lest it should get away. They proceeded to block up their entrance tunnel about three feet from the door. They packed the earth hard, and made a good job of it, and flattered themselves that their guests would not get in in a hurry, even if they were pretty good burrowers themselves. Then at the extreme opposite corner of their central chamber they tunneled a new passageway, which brought them out quite on the other side of the hillock. This done, they felt very pleased with themselves, and settled down for a well-earned sleep, curled up in a furry ball together.

"At daybreak the owls came home. Confidently they ducked their big, round heads and dived down the old entrance, only to be brought up with a bump when they had gone about three feet. Out they came in a rage, fluffing their feathers and snapping their beaks, and stood on each side of the hole to talk the affair over. First, one and then the other reëntered to investigate. They found it quite inexplicable. They felt sure this *was* the way they had previously entered—so sure, in fact, that again and again they tried it, only growing more and more puzzled and indignant with each attempt. Finally they came to the conclusion that they must have made some mistake. They scuttled solemnly round the hillock, and came upon the new entrance. Ah, of course, they *had* been mistaken. Their indignation vanished. They scurried in cheerfully, one hard upon the other's tail, and took up their place in their adopted corner. The Little Villager and his mate opened disgusted eyes upon them for a second, then went to sleep again, relinquishing all thought of further protest.

"After this, for a time, there was perfect peace in the house, the peace of mutual aversion. Hosts and guests ignored each other scrupulously. But after a while a family was born to the Little Villager, a litter of absurd, blind, tiny whimperers, all heads and hungry mouths. The two owls were immensely interested at once, but their efforts to show their interest were met by such an astonishing display of ferocity on the part of both the Little Villager and his mate that they discreetly withdrew their advances and once more kept strictly to themselves. They knew their business, these owls; and they knew they would lose nothing in the long run by a little temporary forbearance. They were well aware, from past experience with prairie dogs, that the vigilance of the happy parents would relax in course of time, and that all the while the little ones, growing larger and plumper every day, would be getting better worth the interest of an appreciative owl.

"The event proved they were right. As the days went by, and the young ones grew lively and independent, the Little Villager and his mate grew less and less anxious about them. Their soft eyes now wide open, they would leave the nest and wander about the burrow, in spite of all that their mother or their father (whichever happened to be in charge at the time) could do to prevent them. There were so many of them, moreover, that it was quite impossible to keep an eye on them all at once.

"Late one afternoon, in that debatable time when the owls in their corner were just beginning to wake up, two of the youngsters ran over quite near them. The temptation was irresistible. There was a light pounce, a light squeak instantly strangled, and *one* of the youngsters, badly frightened, ran back to the mother. The other remained, limp and motionless, in the owl's corner, with a set of steel-like talons clutching it.

"The mother started to the rescue boldly. But the moment she left the rest of the litter the second owl hopped over toward them. She paused in an agony of irresolution. Then she turned and scurried back. She could not sacrifice all for the sake of one. But as she gathered the survivors to her she barked and chattered furious defiance at the murderer. Her clatter brought down the Little Villager himself, and together they hurled all the insults they could think of at the owl, who, however, calmly turned his feathery back upon them and proceeded to devour his easy prey.

"For some days there was renewed vigilance, and the little ones kept close to their parents' side. But the memory of a prairie dog, especially of a young prairie dog, is distinctly short. Soon there was more wandering from the nest, and then a lot of childish racing about the floor of the burrow. Again a youngster went too near the owls' corner and remained there. This time there was no fuss about it, because the slaughter was accomplished quite silently, and the mother did not happen to see. After this there would never be more than two or three days go by without the sudden disappearance of one or another of the litter, which, after all, kept the burrow from becoming too crowded. The youngsters were getting so big by now that their parents began to lose all interest in them. It became time for them to be weaned. But as the interest of the owls had been increasing as that of the parents diminished, it happened by this time that there was not one left to wean. So the duty of the furry little mother, with her silly nose and her big, childish eyes, was singularly simplified. It was no use making more trouble with her unfriendly guests over a matter that was now past remedy. So all was overlooked, and the burrow settled down once more to the harmony of mutual aversion."

Uncle Andy stopped and proceeded to refill his pipe, waiting for the Child's verdict. The Child's face wore the grieved look of one who has had an illusion shattered.

"I shan't ever believe a word Bill tells me again," said he, with injured decision.

"Oh," said Uncle Andy, "you mustn't go so

far as that. Bill tells lots of interesting things that are true enough as far as they go. You must learn to discriminate."

The Child did not know what "discriminate" meant, and he was at the moment too depressed to ask. But he resolved firmly to learn it, whatever it was, rather than be so deceived again.

CHAPTER XII

THE BABY AND THE BEAR

A STIFFISH breeze was blowing over Silverwater. Close inshore, where the Babe was fishing, the water was fairly calm—just sufficiently ruffled to keep the trout from distinguishing too clearly that small, intent figure at the edge of the raft. But out in the middle of the lake the little whitecaps were chasing each other boisterously.

The raft was a tiny one, of four logs pinned together with two lengths of spruce pole. It was made for just the use which the Babe was now putting it to. A raft was so much more convenient than a boat or a canoe when the water was still and one had to make long, delicate casts in order to drop one's fly along the edges of the lily pods. But the Babe was not making long, delicate casts. On such a day as this the somewhat unsophisticated trout of Silverwater demanded no subtleties. They were hungry, and they were feeding close inshore, and the Babe was having great sport. The fish were not large, but they were clean, trim-jawed, bright fellows, some of them not far short of the half-pound; and the only bluebottle in the ointment of the Babe's exultation was that Uncle Andy was not on hand to see his triumph. To be sure, the proof would be in the pan that night, browned in savory cornmeal after the fashion of the New Brunswick backwoods. But the Babe had in him the makings of a true sportsman, and for him a trout had just one brief moment of unmatchable perfection—the moment when it was taken off the hook and held up to be gloated over or coveted.

The raft had been anchored, carelessly enough, by running an inner corner lightly aground. The Babe's weight, slight as it was, on the outer end, together with his occasional ecstatic, though silent, hoppings up and down, had little by little sufficed to slip the haphazard mooring. This the Babe was far too absorbed to notice.

All at once, having just slipped a nice halfpounder onto the forked stick which served him instead of a fishing basket, he noticed that the wooded point which had been shutting off his view on the right seemed to have politely drawn back. His heart jumped into his throat. He turned—and there were twenty yards or so of clear water between the raft and the shore. The raft was gently but none too slowly gliding out toward the tumbling whitecaps.

Always methodical, the Babe laid his rod and his string of fish carefully down on the logs, and then stood for a second or two quite rigid. This was one of those dreadful things which, as he knew, *did* happen, sometimes, to other people, so that he might read about it. But that it should actually happen to *him!* Why, it was as if he had been reading some terrible adventure and suddenly found himself thrust trembling into the midst of it. All at once those whitecaps out in the lake seemed to be turning dreadful eyes his way and clamoring for *him!* He opened his mouth and gave two piercing shrieks which cut the air like saws.

"What's the matter?" shouted a very anxious voice from among the trees.

It was the voice of Uncle Andy. He had

returned sooner than he was expected. And instantly the Babe's terror vanished. He knew that everything would be all right in just no time.

"I'm afloat. Bill's raft's carrying me away!" he replied in an injured voice.

"Oh!" said Uncle Andy, emerging from the trees and taking in the situation. "You *are* afloat, are you! I was afraid from the noise you made that you were sinking. Keep your hair on, and I'll be with you in five seconds. And we'll see what Bill's raft has to say for itself after such extraordinary behavior."

Putting the canoe into the water, he thrust out, overtook the raft in a dozen strokes of his paddle, and proceeded to tow it back to the shore in disgrace.

"What on earth did you make those dreadful noises for?" demanded Uncle Andy, "instead of simply calling for me, or Bill, to come and get you?"

"You see, Uncle Andy," answered the Babe, after some consideration, "I was in a hurry, rather, and I thought you or Bill might be in a hurry, too, if I made a noise like that, instead of just calling."

"Well, I believe," said Uncle Andy, seating himself on the bank and getting out his pipe, "that at last the unexpected has happened. I believe, in other words, that you are right. I once knew of a couple of youngsters who might have saved themselves and their parents a lot of trouble if they could have made some such sound as you did, at the right time. But they couldn't, or, at least, they didn't; and, therefore, things happened, which I'll tell you about if you like."

The Babe carefully laid his string of fish in a cool place under some leaves, and then came and sat on the grass at his uncle's feet to listen.

"They were an odd pair of youngsters," began Uncle Andy—and paused to get his pipe going.

"They were a curious pair, and they eyed each other curiously. One was about five years old and the other about five months. One was all pink and white, and ruddy tan, and fluffy gold, and the other all glossy black. One, in fact, was a baby, and the other was a bear.

"Neither had come voluntarily into this strange fellowship; and it would have been

"He had come to the raft quite uninvited."

hard to say which of the pair regarded the other with most suspicion. The bear, to be sure, at five months old, was more grown up, more self-sufficing and efficient than the baby at five years; but he had the disadvantage of feeling himself an interloper. He had come to the raft quite uninvited, and found the baby in possession! On that account, of course, he rather expected the baby to show her white little teeth, and snarl at him, and try to drive him off into the water. In that case he would have resisted desperately, because he was in mortal fear of the boiling, seething flood. But he was very uneasy, and kept up a whimpering that was intended to be conciliatory; for though the baby was small, and by no means ferocious, he regarded her as the possessor of the raft, and it was an axiom of the wilds that very small and harmless-looking creatures might become dangerous when resisting an invasion of their rights.

"The baby, on the other hand, was momentarily expecting that the bear would come over and bite her. Why else, if not from some such sinister motive, had he come aboard her raft, when he had been traveling on a perfectly good tree? The tree looked so much more interesting than her bare raft, on which she had been voyaging for over an hour, and of which she was now heartily tired. To be sure, the bear was not much bigger than her own Teddy Bear at home, which she was wont to carry around by one leg, or to spank without ceremony whenever she thought it needed discipline. But the glossy black of the stranger was quite unlike the wild and grubby whiteness of her Teddy, and his shrewd little twinkling eyes were quite unlike the bland shoe buttons which adorned the face of her uncomplaining pet. She wondered when her mother would come and relieve the strain of the situation.

"All at once the raft, which had hitherto voyaged with a discreet deliberation, seemed to become agitated. Boiling upthrusts of the current, caused by some hidden unevenness on the bottom, shouldered it horridly from beneath, threatening to tear it apart, and unbridled eddies twisted it this way and that with sickening lurches. The tree was torn from it and snatched off reluctant all by itself, rolling over and over in a fashion that must have made the cub rejoice to think that he had quitted a refuge so eccentric in its behavior. As a matter of fact, the flood was now sweeping the raft over what was, at ordinary times, a series of low falls, a succession of saw-toothed ledges which would have ripped the raft to bits. Now the ledges were buried deep under the immense volume of the freshet. But they were not to be ignored, for all that. And they made their submerged presence felt in a turmoil that became more and more terrifying to the two little passengers on the raft.

"There was just one point in the raft, one only, that was farther away than any other part from those dreadful, seething-crested black surges—and that was the very center. The little bear backed toward it, whimpering and shivering, from his corner.

"From her corner, directly opposite, the baby too backed toward it, hitching herself along and eyeing the waves in the silence of the terror. She arrived at the same instant. Each was conscious of something alive, and warm, and soft, and comfortable—with motherly suggestion in the contact. The baby turned with a sob and flung her arms about the bear.

The bear, snuggling his narrow black snout under her arm as if to shut out the fearful sight of the waves, made futile efforts to crawl into a lap that was many sizes too small to accommodate him.

"In some ten minutes more the wild ledges were past. The surges sank to foaming swirls, and the raft once more journeyed smoothly. The two little voyagers, recovering from their ecstasy of fear, looked at each other in surprise—and the bear, slipping off the baby's lap, squatted on his furry haunches and eyed her with a sort of guilty apprehension.

"Here it was that the baby showed herself of the dominant breed. The bear was still uneasy and afraid of her. But she, for her part, had no more dread of him whatever. Through all her panic she had been dimly conscious that he had been in the attitude of seeking her protection. Now she was quite ready to give it—quite ready to take possession of him, in fact, as really a sort of glorified Teddy Bear come to life; and she felt her authority complete. Half-coaxingly, but quite firmly, and with a note of command in her little voice which the animal instinctively understood, she said: 'Tum here, Teddy!' and pulled him back unceremoniously to her lap. The bear, with the influence of her comforting warmth still strong upon him, yielded. It was nice, when one was frightened and had lost one's mother, to be cuddled so softly by a creature that was evidently friendly, in spite of the dreaded man smell that hung about her. His mother had tried to teach him that that smell was the most dangerous of all the warning smells his nostrils could encounter. But the lesson had been most imperfectly learned, and now was easily forgotten. He was tired, moreover, and wanted to go to sleep. So he snuggled his glossy, roguish face down into the baby's lap and shut his eyes. And the baby, filled with delight over such a novel and interesting plaything, shook her yellow hair down over his black fur and crooned to him a soft, half-articulate babble of endearment.

"The swollen flood was comparatively quiet now, rolling full and turbid over the drowned lands, and gleaming sullenly under a blaze of sun. The bear having gone to sleep, the baby presently followed his example, her rosy face falling forward into his woodsy-smelling black fur. At last the raft, catching in the trees of a submerged islet, came softly to a stop, so softly as not to awaken the little pair of sleepers.

"In the meantime two distraught mothers, quite beside themselves with fear and grief, were hurrying downstream in search of the runaway raft and its burden.

"The mother of the baby, when she saw the flood sweeping the raft away, was for some moments perilously near to flinging herself in after it. Then her backwoods common sense came to the rescue. She reflected, in time, that she could not swim—while the raft, on the other hand, could and did, and would carry her treasure safely enough for a while. Wading waist deep through the drowned fields behind the house, she gained the uplands, and rushed dripping along the ridge to the next farm, where, as she knew, a boat was kept. This farmhouse, perched on a bluff, was safe from all floods; and the farmer was at home, congratulating himself. Before he quite knew what was happening, he found himself being dragged to the boat—for his neighbor was a strenuous woman, whom few in the settlement presumed to argue with, and it was plain to him now that she was laboring under an unwonted excitement. It was not until he was in the boat, with the oars in his hands, that he gathered clearly what had happened. Then, however, he bent to the oars with a will which convinced even that frantic and vehement mother that nothing better could be demanded of him. Dodging logs and wrecks and uprooted trees, the boat went surging down the flood, while the woman sat stiffly erect in the stern, her face white as death, her eyes staring far ahead, while from time to time she muttered angry phrases which sounded as if the baby had gone off on a pleasure trip without leave and was going to be called to sharp account for it.

"The other mother had the deeper and more immediate cause for anguish. Coming to the bank where she had left her cub in the tree, she found the bank caved in and the tree and cub together vanished. Unlike the baby's mother, she *could* swim; but she knew that she could run faster and farther. In stoic silence, but with a look of piteous anxiety in her eyes, she started on a gallop down the half-drowned shores, clambering the heaps of débris, and swimming the deep, still estuaries where the flood had backed up into the valleys of the tributary brooks.

"At last, with laboring lungs and pounding heart, she came out upon a low, bare bluff overlooking the flood, and saw, not a hundred yards out, the raft with its two little passengers asleep. She saw her cub lying curled up with his head in the baby's arms, his black fur mixed with the baby's yellow locks. Her first thought was that he was dead—that the baby had killed him and was carrying him off. With a roar of pain and vengeful fury, she rushed down the bluff and hurled herself into the water.

"Not till then did she notice that a boat was approaching the raft—a boat with two human beings in it. It was very much nearer the raft than she was—and traveling very much faster than she could swim. Her savage heart went near to bursting with rage and fear. She knew those beings in the boat could have but one object—the slaughter, or at least the theft, of her little one. She swam frantically, her great muscles heaving as she shouldered the waves apart. But in that race she was hopelessly beaten from the first.

"The boat reached the raft, bumped hard upon it—and the baby's mother leaped out while the man, with his boathook, held the two craft close together. The woman, thrusting the cub angrily aside, clutched the baby hysterically to her breast, sobbing over her and muttering strange threats of what she would do to her when she got her home to punish her for giving so much trouble. The baby did not seem in the least disturbed by these threats—to which the man in the boat was listening with a grin—but when her mother started to carry her to the boat she reached out her arms rebelliously for the cub.

" 'Won't go wivout my Teddy Bear,' she announced with tearful decision.

" 'Ye'd better git a move on, Mrs. Murdoch,' admonished the man in the boat. 'Here's the old b'ar comin' after her young un, an' I've a notion she ain't exactly ca'm.'

"The woman hesitated. She was willing enough to indulge the baby's whim, the more so as she felt in her heart that it was in some respects her fault that the raft had got away.

She measured the distance to that formidable black head cleaving the waters some thirty yards away.

" 'Well,' said she, 'we may's well take the little varmint along, if baby wants him.' And she stepped over to pick up the now shrinking and anxious cub.

" 'You quit that an' get into the boat quick!" ordered the man in a voice of curt authority. The woman whipped round and stared at him in amazement. She was accustomed to having people defer to her; and Jim Simmons, in particular, she had always considered such a mild-mannered man.

" 'Get in!' reiterated the man in a voice that she found herself obeying in spite of herself.

" 'D'ye want to see baby et up afore yer eyes?' he continued sternly, hiding a grin beneath the sandy droop of his big mustache. And with the baby kicking and wailing and stretching out her arms to the all-unheeding cub, he rowed rapidly away just as the old bear dragged herself up upon the raft.

"Then Mrs. Murdoch's wrath found words, and she let it flow forth while the man listened as indifferently as if it had been the whistling of the wind. At last she stopped.

"'Anything more to say, ma'am?' he asked politely.

"Mrs. Murdoch snorted a negative.

"'Then all *I* hev to say,' he went on, 'is that to *my* mind *mothers* has *rights.* That there b'ar's a mother, an' she's got felin's, like you, an' she's come after her young un, like you—an' I wasn't a-goin' to see her robbed of him.'"

CHAPTER XIII

THE LITTLE SLY ONE

FROM away up near the top of the rocky hill that rose abruptly across the inlet came a terrible screech, piercing and startling.

"Gee!" said the Babe, slipping closer to Uncle Andy, where they sat together on a log by the water. "I'm glad that's away over there! What is it, Uncle Andy?"

"Lynx!" replied Uncle Andy, puffing at his pipe.

"What did he go and do *that* for?"

"Well," said Uncle Andy presently, "if you'll try your level best to listen without interrupting, I'll tell you."

"I'm *not* interrupting!" protested the Babe.

"Of course not!" agreed Uncle Andy. "Well, you see, the lynx is the slyest thing that goes on four legs. You think, maybe, a fox is sly. That fool guide Bill's told you that. Now, a fox is sly when he chooses to be, and

when he wants to be impudent he'd sass King Solomon to his face. But a lynx is just born sly, and can't even think of outgrowing it."

"I don't see anything *sly* about that noise he made just now!" said the Babe.

"There you go!" exclaimed Uncle Andy. Then he stopped and thought for quite a while. But as the Babe never spoke a word he soon went on again.

"You see, I was just coming to that. That awful screech is one of the slyest things he does. That fellow has been hunting a while without catching anything. Creeping, creeping on his great furry feet, making no more sound than the shadow of the leaf on the moss; for all his quietness he hasn't had any luck. So at last, hiding behind a bush, he let out that screech just to start things moving. Did you notice how quick it stopped? Well, he knew if there was any rabbit or partridge asleep near by it would be so startled it would jump and make a noise; and then he'd be on it before it could more than get its eyes open. Don't you call that sly?"

The Babe merely nodded, being resolved not to interrupt.

"Good," said Uncle Andy. "You're improving a lot. Now, let me tell you, the slyest thing of all is the Little Sly One, which those who know everything call the lynx kitten. The Little Sly One is good enough for us to call her, for she is even slyer when she is a she than when he is a he. Is that quite clear?"

"Of *course!*" exclaimed the Babe.

"Well, the Little Sly One was a lonely orphan. She had had a mother and a sister and two brothers; but a man with a dog and a gun had happened on the mouth of the cave in which they lived. The dog had hastily gone in. There was a terrible noise in the cave all of a sudden, and the dog would have hastily come out again, but for the fact that he was no longer able to come or go anywhere. When the noise had stopped so that he could see in, the man had shot the mother lynx. Then he had shot the dog, because that was the only thing to do. And because he was very sorry and angry about the dog, he also shot the lynx kittens, where they crowded, spitting savagely, at the back of the cave. But there were only three of them at the back of the cave. The Little Sly One, instead of bothering to spit when there were other things more important to be done, had run up the wall and hidden in a crevice, so still she didn't even let her tail twitch. Of course, like all her family, she didn't really have a tail, but merely a little blunt stub, perhaps two inches long. But that stub could have twitched, and wanted desperately to twitch, only she would not let it. She always seemed to think she had a tail, and, if she had had, it would have stuck out so the man could have seen it, the crevice being such a very small one. You see how *sly* she was!

"Of course, the Little Sly One was lonely for the next few days, but she was kept so busy hunting breakfasts, and lunches, and dinners, and suppers that she hadn't time to fret much. She was something like a three-quarters-grown kitten now, except for her having no tail to speak of, and curious, fierce-looking tufts to her ears, and pale eyes so savage and bright that they seemed as if they could look through a log even if it wasn't hollow.

"Also, her feet were twice as big as a kitten's would have been, and her hindquarters were high and powerful, like a rabbit's. Her soft, bright fur was striped like a tiger's—

though by the time she was grown up it would have changed to a light, shadowy, brownish gray, hard to detect in the dim thickets.

"The Little Sly One was *so* sly and so small that she had no difficulty in creeping up on birds and woodmice, to say nothing of grass-hoppers, beetles and crickets. But one day she learned, to her great annoyance, that she was not the only thing in the woods that could do this creeping up. She had been watching a long time at the door of a woodmouse burrow, under a tree, when suddenly she seemed to feel danger behind her. Without waiting to look round, being so sly, she shot into the air and landed on the trunk of a tree. As she madly clawed up it, the jaws of a leaping fox came together with a snap just about three inches behind her, just, in fact, where an ordinary tail would have been. So, you see, her tail really saved her life, just by her not having any!

"Well, when she was safely up the tree, of course she couldn't help spitting and growling down at the hungry fox for a minute or two, while he looked up at her with his mouth watering. Then, however, she curled herself up in a crotch and pretended to go to sleep. And then the fox went away, because he didn't know when she would wake up, and he didn't want to wait! You see how sly she was!

"But once it happened she was not so sly as she might have been. You see, after all, in spite of her fierce eyes, she was still only a *kitten* of a lynx; and she *had* to *play* once in a while. At such times she would pounce on a leaf as if it were a mouse, or just tumble all over herself pretending she had a real tail and was trying to catch it. So, of course, when she happened to pass under a low, bushy branch and caught sight of a slim, smooth, black tip of a tail, no bigger than your little finger, hanging down from it, she naturally couldn't resist the temptation. She pranced up on her hind legs and *clawed* that black tip of a tail—clawed it hard!

"The next instant, before she could prance away again, the *other* end of that slim, black tip swung out of the branch and whipped itself round and round her body, and a black head, with sharp fangs in it, hit her *biff, biff, biff!* on the nose. It was the tail of a black snake she had tried to play with."

"Gee! But she wasn't sly that time!" exclaimed the Babe, shaking his head wisely.

"The black snake wasn't poisonous, of course," continued Uncle Andy, "but his fangs hurt the Little Sly One's nose, I can tell you. But the worst of it was, how he could squeeze! Those black coils tightened, tightened, till the Little Sly One, who in her first fright had set up a terrific spitting and yowling, found she had no breath to waste on noise. Her ribs felt as if they would crack. But, fortunately for her, her teeth and claws were available for business. She fell to biting, and ripping, and clawing, till the black snake realized it was no Teddy Bear he had got hold of. For a minute or two he stood it, squeezing harder and harder. Then he wanted to let go.

"And this, I think, was where he made a mistake. As he relaxed his deadly coils and swung his head round, the Little Sly One struck out with both forepaws at once, and succeeded in catching the hissing, darting head. She caught it fairly, and her long, knife-sharp claws sank in, holding it like a carpenter's vise. The next minute she had her teeth in the back of the snake's neck, chewing and tearing.

"Now, the snake's tail was still around the branch, so he tried furiously to swing the Little Sly One up and crush her against the branch. But she was too heavy and too strong. So he came down, instead, and thrashed wildly among the leaves, trying to get a new grip on her. It was no use, however. He had made too big a mistake. And the next minute he kind of straightened out. The Little Sly One had bitten through his backbone, just behind the head.

"Well, now, you see, she had a good square meal before her. But, being very sly, she first looked all round to see if anyone was coming to dine with her. There was no one in sight, but she knew how curiously things get about sometimes. So she growled, on general principles, grabbed the snake in her teeth, and climbed up the tree so she might eat in peace.

"The tail was no good to eat, so she bit it off and scornfully let it drop. If that black snake hadn't had a tail, he would never have been eaten by a kitten lynx; so the Little Sly One, as she considered this point, and also thought of the fox, said to herself: 'Well, maybe my tail doesn't amount to much, after all. But there doesn't seem to be any luck in tails, anyway.'

"For all that, things in general were keeping her so very, very busy the Little Sly One felt lonely and homesick at times. And especially she felt the need of some kind of a nest which she could call her very own, where she could curl herself up and go to sleep without fear of unpleasant interruptions.

"This sort of thing, as you may imagine, was not to be found every day of the week. Most such places had owners, and the Little Sly One was not yet big enough and strong enough to turn the owners out. If she *had* been big enough—— Well, you see, she hadn't any more conscience than just enough to get along with comfortably.

"One fine day, soon after her adventure with the black snake, her search for a home of her own brought her out into the warm sunshine of a little, deserted clearing. It was an old lumber camp, all grown up with tall grass and flowering weeds. The weeds and grass crowded up around the very threshold of the old gray log cabin.

"The Little Sly One stopped short, blinking

in the strong light and sniffing cautiously. There was no smell of danger—none whatever, but a scent came to her nose that she thought was quite the nicest scent in the world.

"Where did it come from? Oh, there is was—that bunch of dull-green weeds! Forgetting prudence, forgetting everything, she ran forward and began rolling herself over and over in ecstasy in the bed of strong-smelling weeds."

"Catnip!" suggested the Babe.

"Of course!" agreed Uncle Andy impatiently. "What else *could* it be?

"The Little Sly One had never heard tell of catnip, but she knew right off it was something good for every kind of cat. When she had had *quite* enough of it, she felt kind of light and silly, and not afraid of anything. So, as bold as you please, she marched right up to the cabin.

"The door was shut. She climbed upon the roof. There was an old bark chimney, with a great hole rotted in its base. She looked in.

"It was pleasantly shadowy inside, with a musty smell and no sign of danger. She dropped upon a narrow shelf. From the shelf, sniffing and glancing this way and that, she sprang to a kind of wider shelf close under the eaves.

"That was a bunk, of course, where one of the lumbermen used to sleep, though *she* didn't know *that.* It was full of old dry hay, very warmy and cozy. And the hay, as the Little Sly One observed at once, was full of mice.

"She pounced on one at once and ate it. Decidedly, this was the place for her. She curled herself up in the warm hay and went to sleep without fear of any enemies coming to disturb her."

"But what would she do when the lumbermen came back?" demanded the Babe anxiously.

"By *that* time," answered Uncle Andy, putting away his pipe and rising to go, "she would no longer be the *Little* Sly One! She'd be big enough to take care of herself—and run away as soon as she heard them coming."

CHAPTER XIV

THE DARING OF STRIPES TERROR-TAIL

"WHAT would you do if a bear came at you, Uncle Andy?" inquired the Babe.

"Run," said Uncle Andy promptly, "unless I had a gun!"

The Babe thought deeply for a moment.

"And what would you do if a little, teeny, black-and-white striped skunk came at you?" he asked.

"Run like sixty!" responded Uncle Andy, still more promptly.

"But a skunk's so little!" persisted the Babe. "Will he bite?"

"Bite!" retorted Uncle Andy scornfully. "He doesn't have to. It appears to me you don't know skunks very well!"

"Huh!" said the Babe. "I've smelt 'em. But *smells* can't hurt anybody."

"With your notions of skunks," answered Uncle Andy, "you're going to get yourself into a heap of trouble one of these days. I'd better tell you about what happened once when a small young skunk, out walking all by himself in the dewy twilight, happened to meet a large young bear."

Now, the Babe had a great respect for bears.

"Huh!" said he scornfully. "What could *he* do to a bear?"

"The little skunk's name," said Uncle Andy, paying no heed to the interruption, "was Stripes Terror-Tail. He was a pretty fellow, black and glossy, with two clear white stripes down his back on each side of his backbone. His tail was long and bushy, and carried high in a graceful curve; and he was about the size of a half-grown kitten.

"Generally he went hunting with the rest of his family, for the Terror-Tails are affectionate and fond of each other's companionship. But each one does just as he likes, in his easy way; so on this particular evening little Stripes had strolled off by himself over the dewy hillocks, catching fat crickets in the dim twilight, and hoping every minute that he might find a ground sparrow's nest under some bush."

"Did he rob birds' nests?" asked the Babe,

remembering that this, for boys, was one of the deadly sins.

"He certainly did!" said Uncle Andy, who didn't like to be interrupted. "That is, when he had a chance. Well, as luck would have it, a young bear was out nosing around the hillocks that evening, amusing himself with the fat crickets. He wasn't very hungry, being chock full of the first blueberries.

"He would sit back on his haunches, like a tremendous, overgrown black puppy, with his head tilted to one side, his ears cocked shrewdly, and a twinkle in his little dark eyes; and with one furry forepaw he would pat a thick bunch of grass till the frightened crickets came scurrying out to see what was the matter. Then he would almost fall over himself trying to scoop them all up at once—and while he was chewing those he'd caught he'd look as disappointed as anything over those that got away.

"Well, when he got tired of crickets he thought he'd look for a bird's nest. He came to a wide, flat, spreading juniper bush, just the kind that might have a bird's nest under it; and as he nosed around it he came face to face with little Stripes. You see, they were both after the same thing, and both had the same idea about the best place to look for it.

"Now, that young bear's education had been terribly neglected. He didn't know any more about skunks than you do. So he thought, maybe the soft little black-and-white thing with the fluffy tail carried so airily might be just as good to eat as birds' eggs—besides being more filling, of course.

"He would have grabbed little Stripes right off, had the latter tried to run away. But as Stripes showed no sign of any such intention, the bear hesitated. After all, there didn't seem to be any great hurry! He put out a big paw to slap the stranger, but changed his mind and drew it back again, the stranger seemed so unconcerned. It was decidedly queer, he thought to himself, that a little scrap of a creature like that should be taking things so easy when he was around. He began to feel insulted.

"As for Stripes, nothing was farther from his mind than running away from the big black creature that had suddenly appeared in front of him. It was not for a plump, leisurely little skunk to be taking violent exercise on a hot night. Yet he didn't want to walk right over the bear—not at all. And he had no intention of making things disagreeable for the clumsy-looking stranger."

"Huh, what could *he* do to *him?*" interrupted the Babe again. He had the greatest faith in bears.

"*Will* you wait!" groaned Uncle Andy. "But first let me explain to you the peculiar weapon with which Stripes, and all the Terror-Tail family, do their fighting when they have to fight—which they are quite too polite to do unnecessarily. Some distance below his bushy, graceful tail, sunken between the strong muscles of his thighs, Stripes had a shallow pit, or sac, of extraordinarily tough skin containing a curious gland which secreted an oil of terrible power.

"The strong muscles surrounding this sac kept the mouth of it always so tightly closed that not an atom could get out to soil the little owner's clean, dainty fur, or cause the slightest smell. In fact, Stripes was altogether one of the cleanest and daintiest and most gentlemanly of all the wild creatures. But when he *had* to, he could contract those muscles around the oil sac with such violence that the deadly oil—blinding and suffocating—would be shot forth to a distance of several feet, right into the face of the enemy. And *that,* let me tell you, was never good for the enemy!"

"Why?" demanded the Babe.

But Uncle Andy only eyed him scornfully.

"When Stripes, quite civilly, looked at the bear, and then proceeded to smell around under the juniper bush for that bird's nest, which didn't seem to be there, the bear was much puzzled. He put out his paw again—and again drew it back.

"Then he said 'Wah!' quite loud and sharp, to see if that would frighten the imperturbable stranger. But Stripes didn't seem to mind noises like that. His bright, intelligent eyes were on the bear all the time, you know, though he seemed to be so busy hunting for that bird's nest.

" 'Pooh!' said the bear to himself, 'he's just plain idiot, that's what's the matter with him. I'll eat him, anyway!' and he bounced forward, with paw uplifted, intending to gather Stripes as he would a fat cricket."

Here Uncle Andy was so inconsiderate as to

pause and relight his pipe. The Babe clutched his arm.

"Well," he went on presently, "just at this moment Stripes made as if he was going to run away, after all. He whisked round and jumped about two feet, and his fine tail flew up over his back, and in that very instant the bear thought the whole side of the hill had struck him in the face.

"He stopped with a bump, his nose went straight up in the air, and he squalled: 'Wah-ah! Wah——' But in the middle of these remarks he choked and strangled and started pawing wildly at his nose, trying to get his breath.

"His eyes were shut tight, and that deadly oil clung like glue. His paws couldn't begin to get it off, and so he fell to rooting his nose in the turf like a pig, and plowing the grass with his whole face, fairly standing on his head in his efforts, all the time coughing and gurgling as if he was having a fit.

"His behavior, in fact, was perfectly ridiculous; but there was no one there to laugh at it but Stripes, and he was too polite. He just strolled on quietly to another bush, and kept looking for that bird's nest.

"At last the bear, what with pawing and rooting, managed to get his breath and open his eyes. He wallowed a bit more, and then sat up, his nose full of dirt, and moss and grass hanging all over his face. He was a sight, I tell you! And how he did dislike himself!

"As he sat there, thinking how he'd ever get away from himself, he caught sight of Stripes, strolling off quietly over the brown hillocks. Sitting back on his haunches, he blinked at the little, leisurely black-and-white figure.

"'And to think I was going to eat *that!*' he said to himself sadly."

"She swam frantically."

CHAPTER XV

DAGGER BILL AND THE WATER BABIES

"WHAT'S that?" demanded the Babe nervously, as a peal of wild, crazy laughter rang out over the surface of the lake.

"Why, don't you know what *that* is yet?" said Uncle Andy with a superior air. "That's old Dagger Bill, the big black-and-white loon. Sounds as if he was terribly amused, doesn't he? But he's only calling to his big black-and-white mate, or the two little Dagger Bills they hatched out in the spring."

"What does *he* do?" asked the Babe.

"I don't *know* much about that fellow," answered Uncle Andy. "Now you see him, and now you don't. Mostly you don't; and, when you do, as likely as not it's only his snaky black head, with its sharp dagger of a bill, stuck up out of the water to keep track of you. He's *most* unsociable. If anyone tells you he knows all about a loon, you wink to yourself and pretend you are not listening. But I'll tell you who *do* know something about old Dagger Bill —the Water Babies.

"Who're the Water Babies?" demanded the Babe.

"Why don't you know *that?* The little muskrats, of course, that live in the warm, dry, dark nest under the dome of their mud house, out in the water—the house with its doors so far under water that no one can get into it without diving and swimming."

"It must be cozy and awfully safe," said the Babe, who began to want a place like that himself.

"Yes, *fine!*" agreed Uncle Andy. "And safe from everything but the mink; and if *he* came in by one door, there was always another door open for them to get out by, so quick that the mink could never see their tails.

"Old Dagger Bill, of course, could never get into the house of the Water Babies, for all his wonderful swimming and diving, because he was so big—as big as a goose. But, as a rule, he wouldn't want to bother the Water Babies. Fish were much more to Dagger Bill's taste than young muskrat; and he could swim so fast under water that few fish ever escaped him, once he got after them.

"This summer, however, things were different at Long Pond. Hitherto it had fairly swarmed with fish—lake trout, suckers, chub, red fins, and so on. But that spring some scoundrel had dynamited the waters for the sake of the big lake trout. Few fish had survived the outrage. And even so clever a fisherman as Dagger Bill would have gone hungry most of the time had he not been clever enough to vary his bill of fare.

" 'If we can't have all the bread we want,' he said to the family, 'we must try to get along on cake!' "

"Dagger Bill *might* get *bread* from some *camp*," interrupted the Babe thoughtfully, being a matter-of-fact child. "But *what* could he know about *cake*, Uncle Andy?"

"Oh, come on! *You* know what I mean!" protested Uncle Andy, aggrieved at the Babe's lack of a sense of humor. "You're too particular, you are! *You* know bread meant fish with Dagger Bill—and cake meant things like winkles and frogs, and watermice, and—Water Babies, of course!

"Well, you know, it was no joke hunting the Water Babies, for the old muskrats could fight, and would, and did! And after Dagger Bill and his family had breakfasted on two or three Water Babies, there was great excitement in all the muskrat homes.

"Dagger Bill was a new enemy, and they were not quite sure how to manage him. The mink they knew, the fox they knew, and the noiseless, terrible eagle owl, and the swooping hawk. All these they had their tricks for evading. And the savage pike they would sometimes fight in his own element.

"But Dagger Bill, swimming under water like a fish, and spearing them from beneath with the deadly javelin of his beak, this was a new and dreadfully upsetting danger. Furry heads got close together, and there was a terrible lot of squeaking and squealing before anyone could make up his mind what to do. And meanwhile Dagger Bill was feeling quite pleased, because he had found out that Water Babies were good—and safe!—to eat.

"Now the Water Babies, I must tell you, had two nests—one in the waterhouse, a few yards out from shore, and one at the end of the burrow leading up into the dry bank. Their favorite amusement, as a rule, was playing tag in the quiet water around the house, sometimes on the surface, sometimes beneath it. They would catch and nip each other by the tails or the hind legs, and sometimes grapple and drag each other down, for all the world like a lot of boys in swimming—but how they could swim! You'd give your eye teeth to swim like they could."

"Bet your boots, Uncle Andy," agreed the Babe enthusiastically. "Specially *these* teeth, 'cause they're my first, and I'll lose 'em soon, anyway."

"Huh!" grunted Uncle Andy, looking at him suspiciously. "But, as I was saying, the Water Babies *could swim.* They were no match for Dagger Bill, however, who was quicker than a fish. And when Dagger Bill took to hunting Water Babies, it was no longer safe for them to play far from home. They would get themselves well nipped by their relations, I can tell you, whenever they went outside the little patch of shallow water between the house and the bank.

"Now the sharpness of Dagger Bill's eyes

was something terrible. From away across the lake, where no muskrat could see him at all, *he* could see the ripple made by the brown nose of the littlest muskrat swimming. So one day, when the Water Babies were playing tag in what was really, you know, nothing more nor less than their own back yard, he saw the swift ripples and splashes crossing and recrossing—and he laughed! *You* know how he laughed.

"And when the muskrats heard that wild laughter, they bobbed up their furry heads, those in the water; and those on land sat up like squirrels to listen, and all were as delighted as possible because the sound was so very far away! Then the Water Babies all began to play about as boldly as you please, because they knew Dagger Bill was away over at the other side of the lake.

"But do you suppose he really was?

"Not much! The moment he was done laughing he dived, and swam as hard as he could straight across the lake, under water. He swam and he swam, a sharp, black-and-white wedge rushing through the golden deep, as long as he could hold his breath. When he could not hold it a moment longer he came up, stuck his bill just above water, took a long breath, and dived again. He was halfway across the lake when he came up that time. Next time he was *all* the way across; but, being very cunning indeed, he came up under a grassy bank, where his black bill was hidden among the stems.

"He was not more than twenty paces now from the place where the Water Babies were splashing and racing and squeaking, and having such a good time on the smooth, sunny water, under the blue, blue sky. They were very happy. Dagger Bill sank back into the deep water so noiselessly, you would have said it was a shadow sinking. Then he rushed forward like a swordfish, down there in the brown glow, and darted up right into the game of tag.

"He had aimed his cruel thrust at the Water Baby who, at that particular moment, was IT. But, in that same second, as luck would have it, IT caught the one he was pursuing, nipped his tail, and doubled back like lightning to escape getting nipped in return. So, you see, Dagger Bill missed his aim. That javelin of his beak just grazed the brown tip of IT's nose, scaring him to death, but nothing more."

"Ah-h!' breathed the Babe, relieved in his feelings.

"In a wink, of course," went on Uncle Andy, "all the Water Babies, with a wild slapping of tails on the water to warn each other, were scurrying desperately for the nest. Some dived as deep as possible; but others lost their wits and swam on the surface. A moment more, and Dagger Bill, who had sunk at once, darted up again, and this time his terrible beak pierced right through a little swimmer's body, severing the backbone."

"Oh-h-h!" murmured the Babe, drawing in his breath sharply.

"I can't help it," said Uncle Andy. "But that's the way things go. Well, now, Dagger Bill rose right out on top of the water, as a bird should, and swam toward shore with the victim hanging limply from his beak. But every old muskrat, along the bank or around the waterhouse, had seen and had understood. Those folks that think muskrats and other wild creatures have sense, would have said it was all planned out ahead—it happened so quick. Every muskrat dived like a flash into the water and disappeared.

"Dagger Bill was coolly making for shore, not dreaming that anybody would dare interfere with *him,* when suddenly his black head went up in the air, his great beak opened with a hoarse squawk, and he dropped the dead Water Baby. His dark wings flopped, and his tail was drawn under so violently that he nearly turned over backward. It seemed to him that nothing less than the Great Sturgeon, which lived far down the river, must have grabbed him by the feet."

"Wish it had been!" said the Babe.

"Just you wait!" said Uncle Andy. "Well, the next minute he looked down, and, lo and behold! all the water underneath him was alive with swimming muskrats, darting up and closing in upon him. Three or four already had their sharp teeth in his feet. He was mad and frightened, I can tell you.

"He struggled and flopped, but his short wings could not raise him from the water with those weights fastened upon his feet. Then his black head shot under, and he jabbed savagely this way and that, making dreadful wounds in those soft, furry bodies. But the muskrats never heeded a wound. They swarmed upon their enemy with a splendid, reckless rage. *They'd* teach him to stab Water Babies!

"And they did, too! In a minute or so they had pulled the old robber clean under, where they could all get at him; and, my! you should have seen how the water boiled! But it was only for a minute or two. Then two musk-rats came up, bleeding, but proud as you please, and then two or three more; and they all went ashore to lick their wounds and make their toilets, for, as you may imagine, their hair was somewhat disarranged.

"And then, while they were combing their fur with the claws of their little forepaws, like hands, who should come up but Dagger Bill; but his feet came up first, and he didn't come up far, anyway, and he didn't stir. In fact, he was good and dead—so dead that presently a young chub, and a red-fin, and two sunfish, came up and swam round him curiously.

"You see, they thought they might never have another chance to get such a *good, comfortable* look at a loon, and be able to talk about it afterwards."

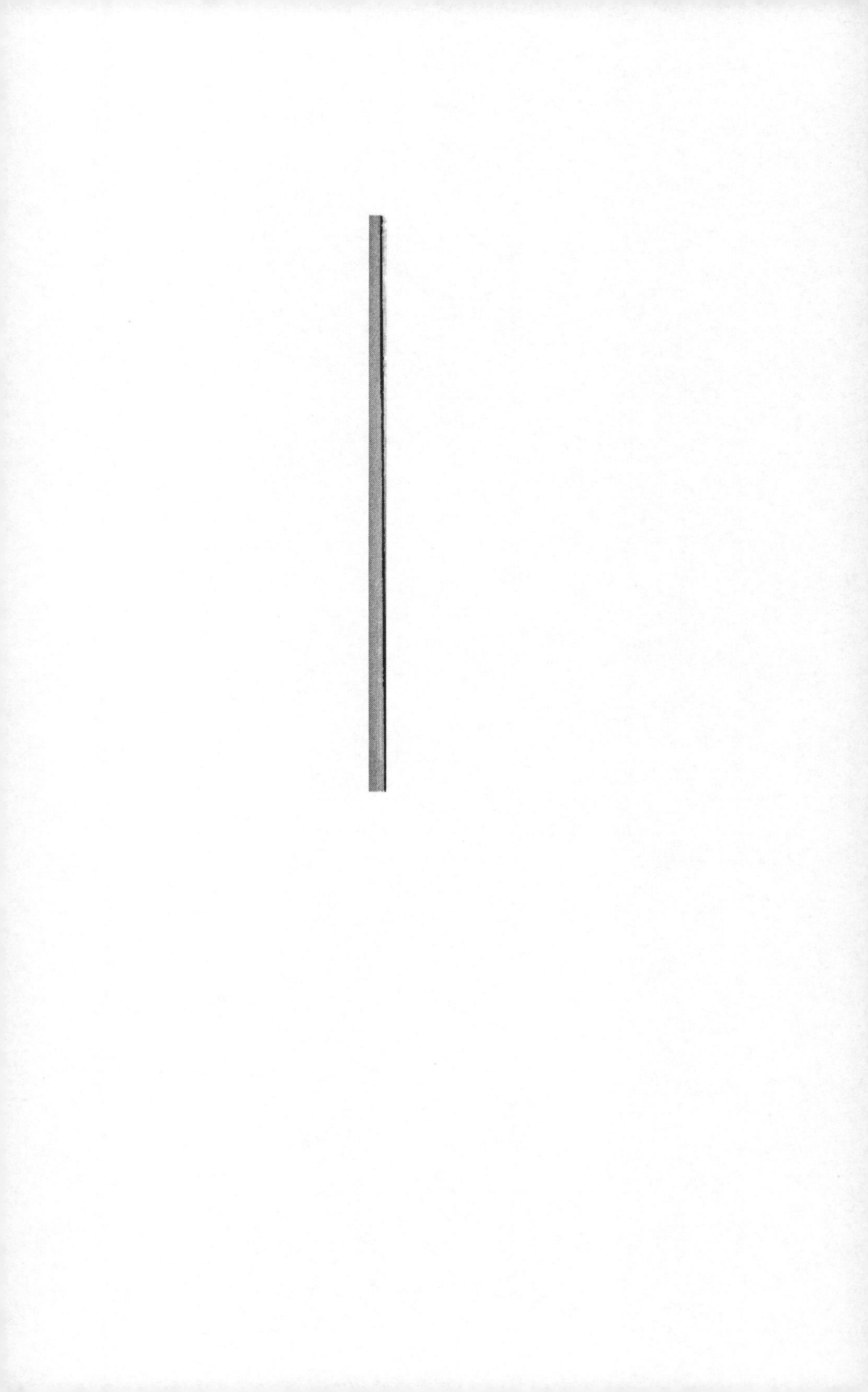

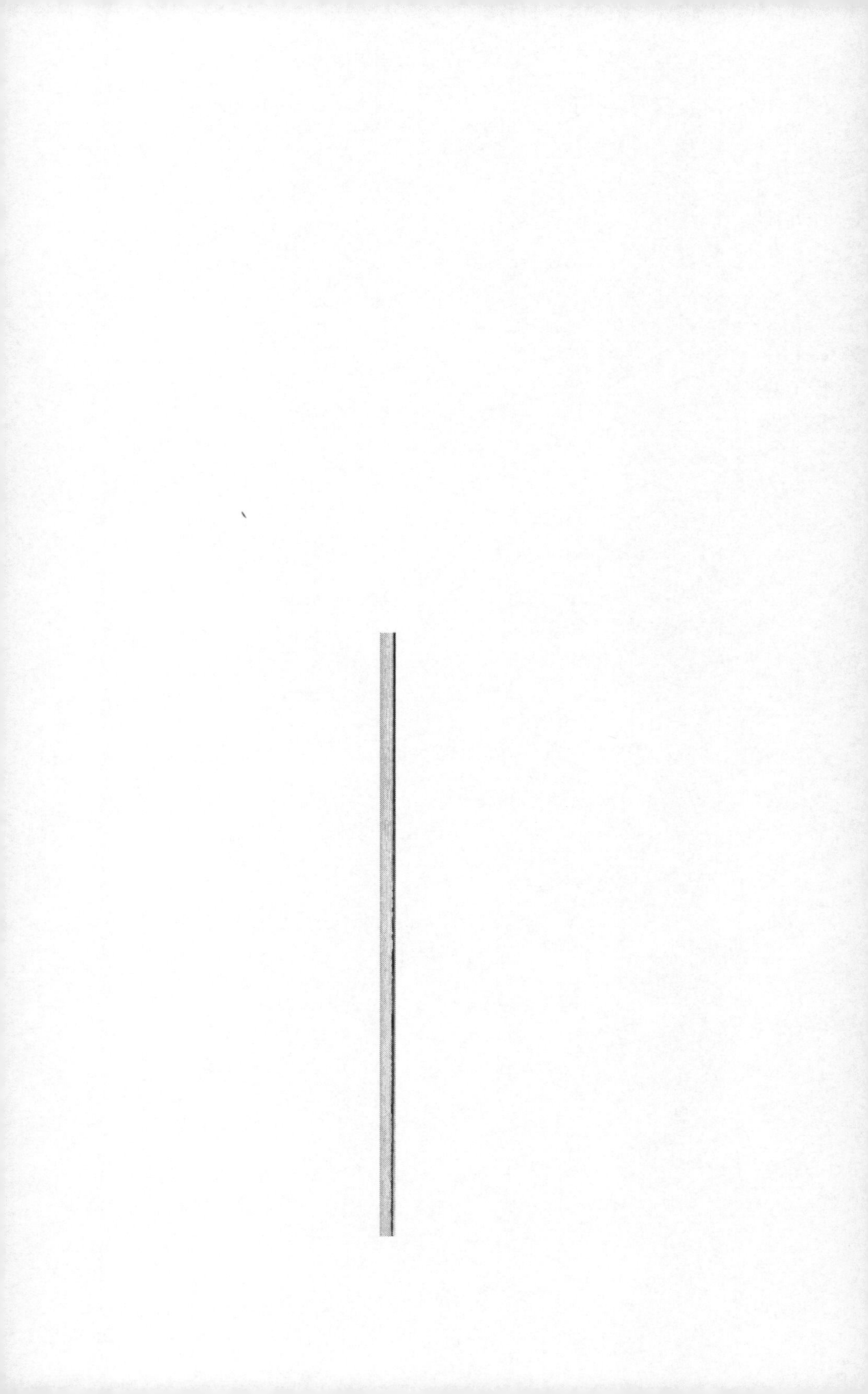

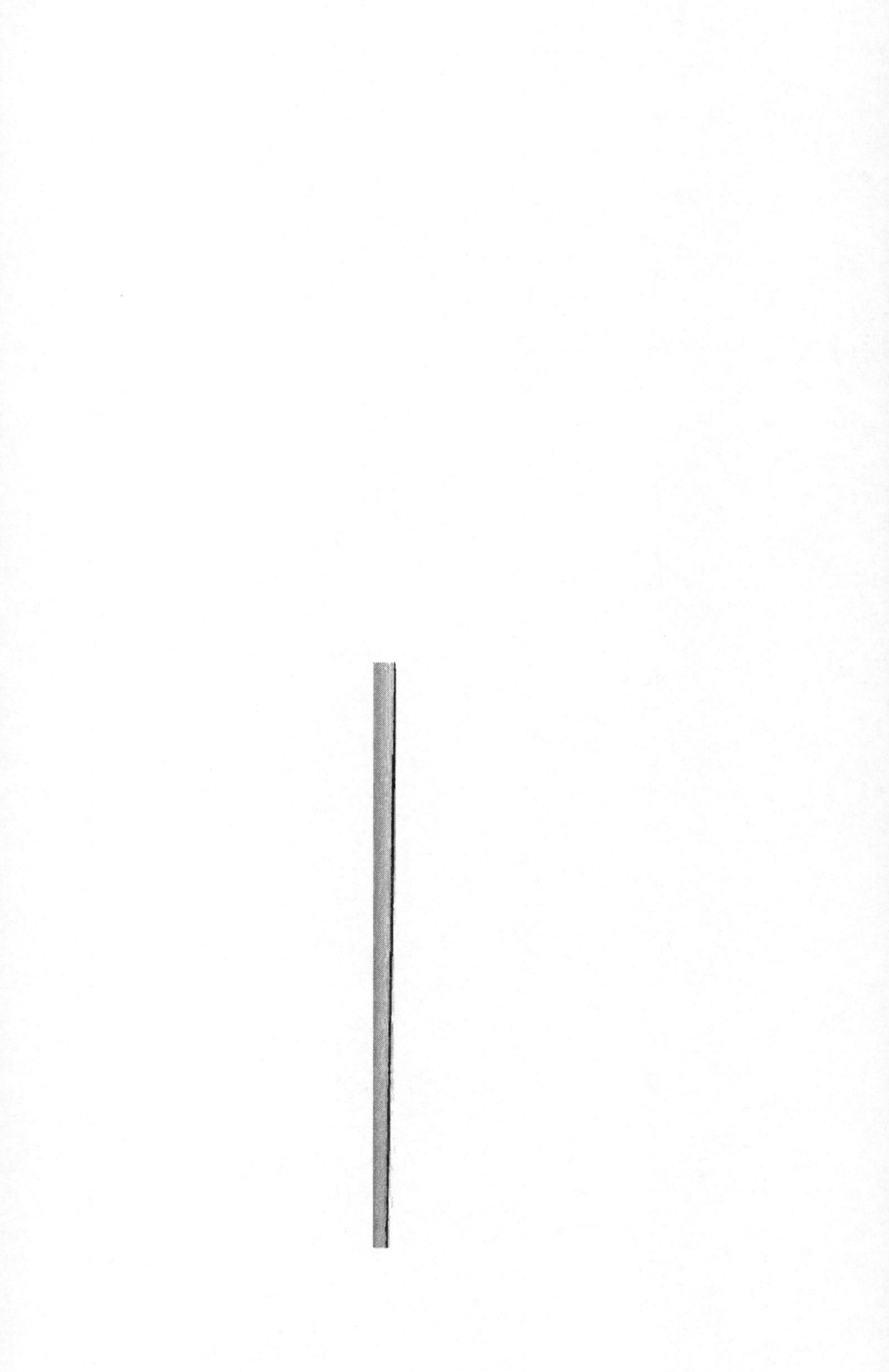

Ingram Content Group UK Ltd.
Milton Keynes UK
UKHW022124060323
418148UK00005B/208